Fly Past

Fly Present

FlyPast

Fly Present

A Celebration of Preserved Aviation

ARMS AND
ARMOUR

Arms & Armour Press
A Cassell imprint
Wellington House, 125 Strand, London WC2R 0BB

Distributed in the USA by Sterling Publishing Co. Inc.,
387 Park Avenue South, New York, NY 10016-8810

Distributed in Australia by Capricorn Link (Australia)
Pty Ltd, 2/13 Carrington Road, Castle Hill, New South
Wales 2154

British Library Cataloguing-in-Publication data:
A catalogue record for this book is available from the
British Library.

ISBN 1 85409 226 X

Edited and designed by Roger Chesneau/DAG
Publications Ltd

Printed and bound in Spain

Title page photographs
Left: Appropriately, this Mustang sports a silhouette
of the animal after which the aircraft is named. The
patriotic spirit that pervades Confederate Air Force
activities is also apparent at this 1989 Harlingen air
show. (Philip Handleman)
Right: A lovely example of the Stearman trainer.
(William Jesse)

Contents

Introduction

Walter Boyne

As we all plunge recklessly up the on-ramps to the information superhighway of the future, with its promised deluge of entertainment, data and synthetic participation, it is comforting to look to the past, to our aviation heritage, to find some truly enduring values. In a world in which national boundaries change more quickly than the cartographers can record them, where supposedly great, stable states like the Soviet Union dissolve overnight, where concepts of employment, health and even morality fluctuate like lines on some berserk oscilloscope, it is essential to find a factor that is constant and unwavering. That constant is the perpetual endeavour found in aviation's history to improve the breed. The field of aeronautics is solidly based on the best efforts of teams of human beings who, year after year, decade after decade, try earnestly and to the utmost of their ability to advance the state of the art.

No one, from before the time of the Wright Brothers until the present, has ever deliberately sought to make an aircraft that is merely ordinary – 'good enough for government work'. The essence of flight lies in overcoming nature, and, to do so, the equipment has to be as near perfect as possible. This is not to say that all aircraft through history have been perfect creations – they have not. But their failings have always been in execution and never in intent. From Langley's valiant if futile attempts on the Potomac to the tension of every flight of the Space Shuttle, the people who design, build, service and fly aircraft do so with every ounce of skill at their disposal.

Below: Used in both the European and the Pacific Wars, the North American B-25 Mitchell was a mainstay of the medium bombing capacity of the Allied airforces. Silver Lady *carries the very early US national insignia, soon changed to avoid confusion with the Japanese 'meatball'. (William Jesse)*

Above: Fairey Swordfish W5856 takes to the air following is restoration at the British Aerospace factory at Brough, May 1993. (BAe)

Amplifying this comforting thought concerning constancy of effort is the fact that aviation has been a miracle of progress, a record of continual improvement along increasingly divergent paths. Advances in aviation have been like an expanding pyramid, a tree, with each branch dividing along new and unexpected lines, always reaching out to new developments, with these in turn subdividing and leading to new areas of improvement.

In the early years of aviation each designer attempted to advance the art by setting new records. The increments of improvement were sometimes small, occasionally dramatic, and only rarely, in later years with planes like the Comet, the B-47 and the SR-71, did they represent a giant leap. The greatest improvements in aircraft technology, sad to say, have often come as a result of the pressures of war, when sufficient funds are available to meet desperate needs and aircraft are produced in enormous quantities.

It is at this point that the concept of preserving the past becomes even more important, for with the pressure of war

totally new methods of construction and production are adopted, setting precedents that continue into peacetime. Progress comes to mean more than an advance in the shape of a fuselage or the power of an engine: it can also be measured in the methods of assembly, even in such mundane things as the choice of a fastener, a paint or an adhesive. Behind each of these individual elements there grows up an industrial culture, a discipline in which craftsmen practise their arts – and it is these arts as well as the artefacts that the modern restoration movement seeks to preserve.

We can be proud to say that the aviation ethic, the need to produce the very best, is still with us. Today, more than nine decades after the Wright Brothers' flight at Kitty Hawk, eight after the First World War and, incredibly, five after the Second, aircraft manufacturers, from those working with home-built kits to the modern giants like British Aerospace, Boeing and Aérospatiale, continue to vie for the honour of creating the best.

It is possible to honour this continual progress by means of books, television

and film, and it is fitting that this is done. But the most rewarding way to remember the efforts of the hundreds of thousands of men and women who have devoted their lives to aviation is by preserving and restoring not only their products but also their skills and crafts. Even the best book or film of the Sopwith Camel cannot impart the excitement of hearing a real Clerget running, of smelling the heady combination of dope and exhaust fumes or of seeing the quick, soaring take-off. Really to understand the Battle of Britain, to get the sense of how fragile the moment was, one has to see a Spitfire in flight, its delicate lines enhanced by the song of its Merlin. The restoration of vintage aircraft preserves these sensations for new generations who would otherwise never know their beauty nor learn of their importance.

Military aircraft are not the only ones to impart the lessons of the past, however. Civilian Jennies inspired an adolescent America to fly: a Curtiss JN-4 would land in a wheatfield and young men and women would determine their careers on the spot. Today our young people are naturally jaded: flights in jets are commonplace, and the concern is not about the thrill but about the food. It is important to get these same young people back to the airports, to see and smell and feel a Jenny, to run their hands over the glistening fabric of a Tiger Moth, to feel the cool, hard metal of a Ryan ST. And we need to get them to do more than look – the skills that our fathers passed on to us must be preserved for the next generation. We need to create the positive excitement of beginning a project and carrying it through to completion, to experience

Left: One of a growing number of restoration projects involving aircraft of the 'Cold War' era – a superb North American F-86 Sabre. (William Jesse)
Below: Zero project: restoration work on the empennage of this Japanese fighter has begun but the forward section has yet to receive attention. (Michael Burr)

again that great moment of truth when the wheels leave the ground. We owe it to those who gave us the great aircraft of the past; we owe it to ourselves; and, most especially, we owe it to the future.

Fortunately, the science and practice of restoration is undergoing fantastic growth – a development that would not have been believed even ten years ago. From being the preserve of museums and a few pioneers like the late Cole Palen, Wally Beery and Jack Barber, the hobby has grown into a miraculous industry in the United States, Great Britain and elsewhere, including countries formerly behind the Iron Curtain. The seminally important Experimental Aircraft Association Fly-In at Oshkosh sees hundreds of warbirds, antiques and clas-

sics of every type. The Confederate Air Force has spawned friendly competitors around the world, all dedicated to the restoration of aircraft and to the concept of a 'flying museum'. There are, increasingly, efforts to build classic aircraft and warbirds from original drawings. While the concept of a new Waco, factory fresh and ready for flight, is staggering, what about the creation of a production line for Yak-3s, or Grumman F3Fs, or Messerschmitt Me 262s – all realities in the 1990s?

In a similar way, there are no longer any holds barred in retrieving aircraft, whether they be buried beneath tons of ice in Greenland, resting deep in the ocean or hidden in the undergrowth of a South Pacific jungle. If they are there, they are identified, sought out and brought back to life and flight. While the chances of finding an aircraft in, say, a barn have diminished, who would believe that a clutch of First World War Halberstadts could be found in an attic? Such events make the mythical underground hangar near Tempelhof, with its still-preserved Focke-Wulf 190s and Me 262s, a dream worth pursuing, no matter what the odds. The world of restoration has in fact reached the point where the only thing that cannot be said is, 'It's impossible!'

And that is part of the lure. As long as someone dreams of what has not yet been done, the restoration movement will continue to flourish. Not every project can involve a rare fighter from the past – the restored Puss Moth can bring as much pleasure to its owner and his friends. The important thing is to continue the process, to keep reaching into the past to learn, and, in doing so, to teach.

The Century of Aviation

Walter Boyne

It didn't begin at Kitty Hawk. The love of flight began countless centuries ago, when the first of the human race looked up to envy the birds. All through the years, this inveterate desire to fly expressed itself in myth, legend and more: many sought to fly in different ways, from the unsuccessful tower-jumpers to the delighted balloonists who begat a still growing sport.

Given human ingenuity, which over the years produced great cathedrals and great ships, huge dams, enormous fortifications, incredible works of art and mechanical marvels like the clock, the printing press, the steam engine and the cotton gin, it is surprising that no successful glider evolved before Sir George Cayley's pioneering effort in 1804. The materials, the tools and the knowledge were all available: all that was lacking was the insight to integrate these factors that only a man like Cayley could provide.

Yet progress was glacial, and eighty-seven years elapsed from Cayley's successful, five-foot wing span model to Otto Lilienthal's first tentative flight with his glider No 3 of 1891. Lilienthal did much to advance the discipline over the next five years, until his death in 1896 in one of his standard No 11 monoplane hang gliders.

Think of it: eighty-seven years from Cayley to Lilienthal. Then, starting with the Wright Brothers' first flights at Kitty

Right: *The Vought F4U Corsair was possibly the greatest carrier fighter of the Second World War and certainly one of the most distinctive. Although over 12,000 were built, comparatively few survive today. (William Jesse)*

Below: *Oshkosh 1993: one of many Stearmans attending the show, in US Army training colours of blue fuselage and yellow wings, with a candy-striped rudder. (Philip Handleman)*

Hawk on 17 December 1903, cast forward another eighty-seven years and consider the bewildering cascade of aeronautical progress. The difference is astronomic – and the word is used advisedly, because in that eighty-seven-year span aviation went from the earth to the moon and beyond.

We are all fortunate beyond measure to have been part of this vast pattern of progress, a pattern which has exceeded the boundaries of the mere mechanics of flight to influence – and in many instances to determine – enormous changes in politics, economics, sociology, health and, sadly but inevitably, warfare. There are some people still living who have witnessed the entire parade, from the Wrights to the present, and millions more who have been a part of a substantial portion of this progress.

Fly Past, Fly Present

And progress is the important word, the touchstone, for every day since that magic moment at Kitty Hawk has seen aviation move forward. The Wrights themselves gave the first impetus to the process, moving in four short years from their first glider to a true flying machine. They were men in a hurry: if the information they sought didn't exist – and it usually didn't – they found it themselves by intelligent, scientific investigation. When they found the hallowed data from Lilienthal's tables on aerofoils to be suspect, they built a wind tunnel and conducted their own investigations and then created their own formulae (which have held up remarkably well over time). When their glider didn't respond as they thought it should, they altered their controls to create a true three-axis system. When they couldn't find applicable data on marine propellers, they conceived of the propeller as a rotating wing and built their own. The United States was, at the time, at the beginning of its automobile boom, and the Wrights thought that there surely must be available an internal combustion engine of a suitable power-to-weight ratio. There was not, so they designed their own. It was a bravura performance, one that combined innovation and speed in a way that had never been seen before and which would come to characterize an entire industry. Furthermore, it was a performance that was not being approached in any degree by any other experimenter anywhere.

The Wright Flyer should have electrified the world. It did not, because too many inventors before it had cried wolf. Parenthetically, not even the Wrights

themselves seemed to understand the historical importance of their 1903 Flyer. After the aircraft's last flight on 17 December 1903 it was overturned by a gust of wind. Returned still damaged to Dayton, it was left in deplorable storage conditions until 1916 before being hastily, and by today's standards unauthentically, repaired, to be exhibited at the Massachusetts Institute of Technology.

The Wrights had gone on to greater things, demonstrating a practical aircraft in 1905 which they flew openly over Huffman Prairie, but acceptance came only grudgingly from the American public and not at all from the United States military and most foreign observers. It was not until their twin *tour de force* of 1908, when Orville convinced the military at Fort Myer while Wilbur converted

Above: Restored by volunteers, this Fokker Triplane replica is a superb example of the art of refurbishment. (Nicholas Veronico)

the unbelieving in France, that the Wrights received their proper homage. Orville's demonstration at Fort Myers ended in a crash, and in the first death from powered flight, that of Lieutenant Thomas Selfridge, a pilot and inventor himself. Wilbur's demonstration in France ended in an orgy of imitation as European designers raced back to their drawing boards, their heads filled with what they had seen at Le Mans.

In many ways Wilbur's flight was the more important, acting as it did as a catalyst for the hundreds of European aviators who had tried and failed to create an aeroplane. Wilbur's effortless performance let the genie of European talent out of the bottle: after having been openly scorned, the two brothers were first acclaimed, then copied. Through 1909 it had

been Orville or Wilbur Wright setting their own records for endurance, speed and altitude; then, empowered by the Wrights' genius, the Europeans burst upon the scene and competition flowered. There was an aristocratic flair to the European ferment that contrasted strongly with the basic commercial flavour of aviation in the United States. Sportsmen who had been attracted to automobiles (like Louis Blériot and Charles Rolls) now directed their attention to aviation. There was another factor: in Europe, an army officer had cachet, and many sons of noble families held commissions. When some of them became interested in aviation, they were well positioned to influence their governments to back developments with sums of money huge for the time.

13

Fly Past, Fly Present

It was very different in America, where aviation was viewed as a spectator sport like automobile racing, suitable for country fairs and race-track venues but hardly an upper-class pastime. In the United States, Army officers had little respect and less money, and those who wanted to fly did so largely at their own expense. The result was a period of stagnation in respect of aviation in the United States, one that was assisted by the litigious tendency of the Wright Brothers to put defending their patents above further technological advance. The Wrights had proper reason to be concerned about infringement, but the battles with Glenn Curtiss and others dampened their creative spark.

Thus it was that the focus of aviation progress shifted to Europe. There Blériot and Hubert Latham duelled to see who would be first across the English Channel. Blériot's success elated the world, but there were many who realized that Britain was no longer an island as a result. (Latham's failure and the collapse of the Antoinette company he represented impelled him to leave aviation; he later died on safari, trampled to death by a water buffalo.) New names appeared which became famous overnight: Léon Delagrange flew his Blériot aeroplane for over 100 miles; A. V. Roe flew his ultralight triplane; Frederick Handley Page formed a company to build aircraft; and Albert Santos-Dumont diverted his energies from quasi-comic dirigibles to fixed-wing flight.

Just as it had done more over a century before over balloons, the world now went crazy over aeroplanes, in song, story

and art. That this was due in part to the element of danger is undeniable; and pilots and engineers were attracted to the sport – it had not yet become a profession – for the same reason. But there was more than that. Flying held an inherent beauty that appealed directly to the soul. An aircraft, admittedly noisy and even dirty on the ground with its oil-spewing engine and dust-raising propeller, became a thing of exquisite grace once airborne, ethereal and full of promise. The promise was not only for aviators: it was for manufacturers as well, who saw new fields to conquer; for speculators to begin creating wealth – for themselves – with stock ventures in aviation companies; and for the press, which now had a new field of dreams to plough. There was also promise for the military, who had quietly taken note of H. G. Wells' visionary novel of 1901, *War in the Air*.

There were cultural effects too. Women were attracted to flying for the same reason as men and, despite the customs of the time, would not be denied. On both sides of the Atlantic women went for rides, took the controls, gave demonstration flights. They flew in many countries and their names fast became legendary – Harriet Quimby, Elise Deroche, Jane Herveu, Hélène Dutrieu, Hilda Hewlett, Blanche Scott, Mili Beese, Mathilde Moisant. All presaged the Amelia Earharts, Jacqueline Auriols, Jackie Cochrans, Jeana Yeagers and Patty Wagstaffs of the future, just as they presaged a cultural revolution.

Part of the charm of the time was that almost every flight could be a record flight.

No one had flown across the United States before Cal Rodgers did it in 1911; no matter that it took him 49 days – he was the first, and he set the record. He also set the pattern for a hobby that has existed to this day – establishing inter-city speed records.

As for the military, it now had for the first time what it had always dreamed about – a chance to see the other side of the hill. And, because it was the military, that was not enough: it wanted to drop something lethal on the enemy while making sure that he could not repay the favour. As aeroplanes began to flow into military services around the world, there was an immediate attempt to make them useful for something more than visual

Above: Supermarine Spitfire AB910, part of the Battle of Britain Memorial Flight. (Tim Laming)
Right: Warbirds are a major attraction worldwide, particularly in the United States. Gary Meerman's FG-1D Corsair is one of forty surviving airframes of this type, of which fewer than a dozen are regularly flown.

reconnaissance. It was unfortunate that a concept as magnificent as an aircraft came to be put to use in battle; on the other hand, the true aeroplane lover could find comfort in the fact that military flying spurred the development of aviation, advancing the science by decades in just a few short years.

In truth, the aeroplane inspired the military: as soon as an aircraft's performance envelope was extended in one regime it was promptly pushed in another. Eugene Ely foreshadowed the aircraft carrier with his flights in a Curtiss pusher from the *Birmingham* in 1910; Lieutenant Myron S. Crissy (after whom San Francisco's Crissy Field is named) dropped a bomb on a target; Lieutenant Benny Foulois – who taught himself to fly in correspondence with the Wrights and would go on to head the Air Corps – used a radio to receive messages while on Mexican border patrol; and Captain Charles de Forest Chandler fired a machine gun from a Wright Model B (although one wonders what the recoil effect was on the 40mph aircraft!).

But this was only practice. In Tripoli on 22 October 1911 the Italian Captain Carlo Piazza made the first wartime reconnaissance flight and on 1 November Lieutenant Giulio Gavotti made the first combat bombing raid. A year later, in Mexico, the world's first dogfight occurred – only two hired mercenaries with hand guns, and no hits, but air combat just the same. The First World War would provide that opportunity in spades: in short order, every type of military aircraft mission would be performed – reconnaissance, artillery spotting, aerial

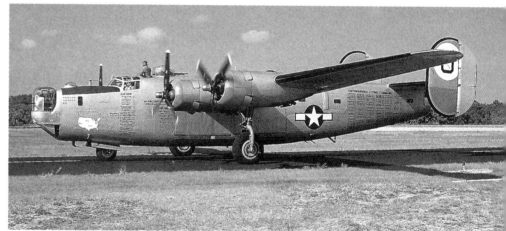

photography, ground strafing, aerial combat, long-range bombing, clandestine operations and the terror bombing of cities.

Under the pressures of war, aircraft grew in strength, speed and carrying capacity. As their performance increased, so did the depth of engineering behind them. Structures that were once gauged by eye and an occasional loading with sandbags were now subjected to intensive testing. A whole new discipline grew up – aeronautical engineering. With the use of slide rules and crude, hand-cranked calculators, structures were evaluated for stress and materials were analyzed for strength, durability and resistance to fatigue. A record-keeping process was established to control the quality of the work – and to apportion blame when that quality was lacking.

Even in the midst of a total revolution in the design and mass manufacture of aircraft, there was still a consistent attempt to achieve the very best with the materials at hand. At Farnborough, Meudon, Adlershof and McCook Field, pilots and engineers worked to produce the superlative. New industries were spawned, new manufacturing methods developed, new production techniques introduced and new management practices evolved.

The growth in military aviation was spectacular in every respect – the funds appropriated for it, the number of types developed, the proliferation of aero-engines, the increasingly sophisticated engineering. A curious equilibrium evolved: the engineers of all the competing nations, no matter what the differences in their resources, managed to come up with aircraft of comparable performance. Thus during the First World War, when the Fokker Eindecker inaugurated what came to be known as the 'Fokker Scourge' by virtue of its machine gun synchronized to fire through the propeller disc, it was quickly countered with the introduction of the Nieuport 11 and the De Havilland D.H.2. These were trumped by the Albatros ace, which was in turn met by the Sopwith Camel, the S.E.5a and the Spad VII. The final German response, the Fokker D.VII, was somewhat delayed, and in the interval the Allies, with their greater resources, introduced new types like the Spad XIII, the Sopwith Snipe and the Bristol F.2B.

Advances in performance were not confined to fighters. Only thirteen years after the Wrights Brothers' first flight there were in service superb aeroplanes of extraordinary performance like the De Havilland D.H.4, the Breguet Br 14 and the Rumpler C.III. The heavy bombers were equally remarkable, from the stalwart Ilya Mourometz on the Eastern Front to the Gothas, Giants and Handley Pages on the Western. No one in 1914, focused on the contemporary B.E.2cs, Taubes and Voisins, could have predicted the size, shape or capability of the aircraft that would be in mass production only three years later.

In assessing these aircraft one tends to think of their beauty of line or of their daring exploits, but truly to understand the century of aviation one also has to look at the engineering and the mechanics behind them. The heart and soul of any aircraft was its engine, which were costly to develop and very demanding of resources. The progress here was astounding: from the Allies' standard 1914 rotary engines of 80 and 100 horsepower or Germany's standard water-cooled 100-horsepower automobile engine there grew a bewildering array of increasingly powerful designs. By the war's end the Allies held the clear advantage in this field because of their seemingly inexhaustible raw materials and fuel. They were able to develop 400-horsepower engines like the Rolls-Royce Eagle and the American Liberty while the German effort was necessarily limited in fighters to Mercedes Benz engines of 160 horsepower or BMW's of 185 and in bombers to heavier engines like the Maybach of 245; these last were in no way competitive with their Allied counterparts.

Yet the Germans often made a virtue of necessity. Limited in the output of their engines, they developed specialized types in order to optimize the resources they possessed. The unequal odds seemed to spur German engineering genius, just as it would do in the Second World War, for from their aircraft factories poured a host of advanced prototypes, including the all-metal Junkers ground-attack planes and the Siemens-Schuckert air-launched missiles.

The advances made during the war provided the basis for civil aviation in the years that followed, where once again competition for records and for national prestige stimulated manufacturers to create outstanding products. They flowed in an endless series, new models emerging annually from around the world from firms whose names had become household words. It was in commercial avia-

tion that the enthusiast's passion was shown, for there was no way to make a profit from an aeroplane without a government subsidy. The world was already well equipped with railways, where fast trains could average 60mph; the oceans were too wide to be spanned by air with passengers or cargo, and the great ships delivered luxury as well as speed on their passage; and, in the United States, the arrival of the mass-produced truck and automobile and the concomitant network of highways created other competitors to the aircraft of the time.

But progress came anyway, at all levels, spearheaded by record flights that

Below: This P-51D Mustang is now based in Switzerland. It was formerly owned by an Eastern Airlines pilot in Nashua, New Hampshire, but is now flown with Swiss Warbirds. (Paul Coggan/ Warbirds Worldwide)

grasped the public imagination and translated into immediate and long-term civil benefits. Thus it was that Lindbergh's epic 1927 flight from New York to Paris gave life and breadth to the reliable radial engine, just as Supermarine's Schneider Trophy racers contributed to the birth of the Merlin. And while the new and increasingly powerful engines were the springboard of progress, designers and inventors sought to bring airframes along with them. The advances rained down – all-metal construction, retractable landing gears, variable-pitch propellers, improved instrumentation, de-icing equipment, superchargers. All

of these were matched by improvements in the infrastructure: airports were built (some even with concrete runways!), navigable air routes were established and services became available at almost every major city.

The mid-1930s were an extraordinarily fertile period the world over as designs like the Messerschmitt Bf 109, Hawker Hurricane, Supermarine Spitfire, Curtiss P-36, Boeing B-17, Heinkel He 111 and Douglas DC-3 emerged, all competing for the relatively small share of the military budgets available at the time. These were the planes in use when the Second World War began, and advanced models of many of these same designs were still fighting six years later when it ended. The nations of the world forgot what they had learned during the First World War. Even in the late summer of 1939, when all hope of peace had disappeared, when the leaders of every nation must have remembered the gigantic scale of the 1918 air forces, contemporary air arms were still very small. With the exception of that of the Soviet Union, these air forces had been scaled down to a level of between one and three thousand aircraft and annual production had been programmed to deliver 500 or 600 planes. Everything was geared down to these spartan levels – training for pilots, observers, mechanics and every other of the many disciplines needed for conflict.

The two principal aggressor nations, Germany and Japan, had created comparatively powerful air forces, exceptionally well trained and intended to be used in surprise attacks. The results they achieved were out of all proportion to the

basic investment. In the ten months from September 1939 to June 1940 Germany's Luftwaffe made possible a series of lightning victories that gave Adolf Hitler possession of most of the European heartland. Japan's even smaller air forces would have a shorter period of conquest, rampaging for just 100 days after 7 December 1941 but creating and empire of even greater area than that of Germany.

However, having had such enormous success combining air power with their other military forces, the two aggressors failed to expand, maintaining production only at the rate necessary to keep their air forces at the level at which they began the war. In contrast, the Allied nations began a frenzy of production which would

wrest dominance of the air from the Axis by 1943. In America alone, where aircraft production had been at the rate of about 3,000 relatively small aircraft a year, output reached 100,000 aircraft a year in 1944. Great Britain's aircraft production surpassed that of Germany in 1940 and remained ahead for most of the rest of the war. The Soviet Union recorded perhaps the greatest success story of all, given that it had to remove its principal factories from Germany's grasp, set them up again and then resume manufacturing. Once again, the process of production in all countries led to social and economic change. Women, particularly in the Allied countries, were given the chance to work in jobs never previously open to

Left: This Yak-3 is on loan from the Yakovlev design bureau to the Museum of Flying at Santa Monica, California. New Yak-3UAs are now being built by Yakovlev from the original tooling for resale. (Nicholas Veronico)
Below: Canberra B.6 XH568 was operated by the Defence Research Agency until 1994, when it was sold to a civilian buyer. Now on the civil register, this unusual aircraft will, it is hoped, be appearing at air shows around Britain. (Tim Laming)

them. The first breaks in the barriers of racial segregation also occurred in America.

Matching this process of expansion and social ferment, a host of revolutionary new aircraft appeared on the scene. The tentative flight of the Heinkel He 178 jet in August 1939 heralded the incredible Messerschmitt Me 262, the first operational jet fighter. Even more extraordinary is the fact that had Frank Whittle been given even modest backing by the British Air Ministry when he first put forward his concept of the jet engine, it is possible that Great Britain would have had fighters so powered in 1939 – the possession of which might well have stayed Germany's hand and prevented the war. As it was, Whittle's efforts made possible the Gloster Meteor and, indirectly, the Lockheed P-80, which would have opposed the Me 262 had the war lasted longer. The

leap forward equivalent to that of jets on the bomber side was the Boeing B-29, a truly extraordinary aircraft that represented a bigger investment – and a bigger risk – even than the Manhattan Project. With an untried airframe, new engines and exotic systems, the B-29 was a gamble that paid off after an agonizing maturing process.

And if during the First World War there had appeared supplementary miracles in support of the aviation programme, in the Second there were a myriad number of them, including vastly improved bomb sights, sophisticated navigation systems, radar, pressurized cabins, air-launched rockets, G-suits, rocket propulsion...the list goes on and on. Less spectacular but definitely as important was the unbelievable logistical system which all air forces had to create to provide airfields, quarters, supplies, parts, maintenance and all

of the millions of elements required to put planes into combat on a regular basis.

The Second World War also saw the helicopter brought to fruition. The first means of flight sought, and for years the most avidly pursued, it was also the most difficult to achieve. Like most new inventions, the helicopter appeared in several countries simultaneously, but it was the German Flettner Fl 282 Kolibri (Humming Bird) and the American Sikorsky R-4 that came into tentative operational use. The war's end naturally terminated the development of the Kolibri, but Sikorsky went from strength to strength, spawning follow-on models and competitors every year. The helicopter's versatility suited it for many missions, none more than air/sea rescue. Begun in earnest during the Korean War, it was carried to a peak of performance in the dismal years of the Vietnam War when the 'Jolly Greens' and their band of support aircraft would go far behind enemy lines to pick up downed flyers. If one seeks nobil-

ity in warfare, it can be found in the search and rescue units.

Commercial aviation had grown prior to the Second World War but had been limited by the types of aircraft available, by the number of airfields around the world (a limitation which had fostered the development of the flying boat) and by a lack of the necessary infrastructure of weather reporting, navigation aids and large-scale maintenance facilities. When the war ended, these were all in place: there were thousands of capable transport aircraft suddenly surplus to requirements and there was scarcely a spot in the world that was not close to a serviceable runway and did not have the minimum radio equipment required. The boom began with a flowering of commercial aircraft. The United States started to assume a dominant role with the immortal Lockheed Constellation, the Douglas DC-4/6/7 series and the Boeing Model 377; Great Britain was quick to respond, with the Vickers Viscount, the first tur-

Above: An illustration of just part of the 1987 Mildenhall Air Fête, featuring no fewer than five aircraft which have now disappeared from the European show scene. The grey-painted F-4C Phantom remains at Mildenhall, suffering at the hands of Battle Damage Repair personnel – what a pity such a beautiful aircraft could not have been preserved. (Tim Laming)

boprop airliner, and the De Havilland Comet, the first jet airliner; and, behind the Iron Curtain the Soviet Union began its expansion of Aeroflot into the world's largest airline, in secrecy of course, and slowly at first.

The jet engine – in combination with the Cold War – gave a mighty impetus to military aviation and new designs emerged from around the world. There was a proliferation of new aircraft from both East and West and the flow from the United States and Great Britain was augmented by brilliant designs from Dassault in France and Saab in Sweden. In today's cramped world, where one type of military aircraft is manufactured by consortia and production runs are limited to a few hundred examples, it is gratifying to recall the days when the major countries would introduce four or five new fighters every decade: the outstanding 'Century Series' comes immediately to mind – the F-100, -102, -104, -105 and -106, all of which had their first flights between 1953 and 1956!

With the jet engines came swept wings, better and safer fuels, in-flight refuelling, advanced avionics for navigation and missile systems, all furthering

Right: The final moments of the Lightning's association with air show crowds as the very last example in RAF service to appear at a British public event taxies out for departure at the 1988 Mildenhall Air Fête. The Lightning was expected to make a come-back during 1994, in civilian hands. (Tim Laming)

the capability to deliver massive numbers of nuclear weapons. The zenith of this frantic expansion in types and numbers may be said to have reached its peak in the West with the introduction of the North American F-86, the Boeing B-47, the Hawker Hunter and the 'V' series of British bombers. Behind the Iron Curtain the pace of production was far greater for the MiG-15 and its successors, along with the bombers that proceeded one after the other down busy Soviet production lines.

At this point a combination of increasing costs and greater performance saw the introduction of progressively fewer new types, procured in fewer numbers and kept in service over protracted periods. Who could possibly have believed at the first flight of the B-52 prototype on 15 April 1952 that its production versions would be in service forty years later, with a ten-year lifespan still predicted? Who would have credited that versions of the Tupolev Tu-20 'Bear', an anomaly at birth as a swept-wing turboprop, would still be droning through the skies, as old, and possibly as capable, as the B-52? And who could possibly have postulated that the unit cost of the Northrop B-2 stealth bomber would climb past $2,000 million, thanks in part to the reduction of its production run to a mere twenty?

Costs were changing the aviation industry of the Western world. Aircraft performance requirements had reached the point where smaller companies could not afford to build prototypes. Companies began to leave the industry. Grand old names that had led the field for years, like Curtiss, Hawker, Blackburn and Martin, either

stopped building aircraft or were merged into larger companies. The process was exacerbated by sudden, irrational government spending cuts which would halt promising programmes just at the moment of their fruition, with no regard for jobs, progress, future contracts or future conflicts: thus were seminal aircraft like the British Aircraft Corporation TSR-2, the Avro CF-105 Arrow and the Martin Seamaster summarily dismissed by politicians who never had to worry about being judged for their actions.

The result has been a coalescing of the number of major manufacturers and, with that, a narrowing of the competition. Despite these changes, however, the last thirty years have seen some of the greatest advances in aviation history. Lockheed, at its incredible 'Skunk Works', produced the U-2, SR-71, F-117 and F-22. Britain and France set an example that would be followed in dozens of future aircraft consortia in creating the incomparable supersonic transport, the Concorde. Boeing has designed and built one money-making transport after another, revolutionizing the world of travel, minimizing the importance of national borders and helping to bring about a global society. The Soviet Union has produced fighters, bombers and transports of superb performance, and in huge numbers by Western standards.

From this avalanche of aircraft there have been myriad spin-offs. One of these is the truly global tourist, each nation providing an identifying kit for its representatives. Exotic places like Nepal, Bali, the Seychelles and Antarctica have suddenly become accessible, not merely to

Below: The awesome Sukhoi Su-27 has become a regular visitor to European air shows, often upstaging many 'home-grown' performers. (Tim Laming)

the *National Geographic* photographer but to everyone. Where once only the elite travelled in German Zeppelins, British Empire flying boats or American clippers, now everyone goes everywhere, and in blue jeans and sandals if that is the wish.

Another fundamentally important development is the use of aircraft for agricultural work. From the primitive 'crop dusters' of the 1920s, putting out their lethal insecticides on the infamous cotton boll weevil, there has grown up a responsible industry using the most prudent products to increase crop yields a hundredfold. Aircraft are used similarly in disease control around the world. The numbers would be difficult to establish,

but there is no question that the number of lives aircraft have saved through the increase in crops and the control of disease exceeds by many thousands of times all those which have been lost to aircraft in warfare.

The aircraft has revolutionized the battlefield, from the first reconnaissance flights that spotted the German Army's progress through France in 1914 to the stealth bomber armed with smart bombs in the Gulf War. It has revolutionized the world's societies: for example, the aeroplane played an important part in the unhinging of the Soviet Union, for mass travel made it impossible to keep the truth of the rest of the world concealed from its people. It has revolutionized business by bringing about a global economy that daily becomes more integrated. And it has revolutionized the attitudes of individuals, who no longer consider distance an impediment to their business or their pleasure.

There is indeed a vast difference in performance between the Wright Flyer's creaking, 120-foot first flight and the supersonic transport, and between Captain Piazza's tentative reconnaissance and the awesome capability of the B-2. But, huge as these differences are, the changes that aviation has fostered around the world are no less so. Had it not been for the requirements of air and space craft, the computer revolution that now holds the world in its grip would have been delayed for decades – indeed, it might never have evolved.

One thing is for sure: we can be thankful for the aeroplane and its effect upon our lives.

The Phenomenon of Flight

Walter Boyne

On any sunny Saturday afternoon you can find genial crowds of people parked near the approach end of the runway at a large airport. Some come with picnic lunches, others with notebooks to record the tail numbers, still others with just a look of longing in their eyes, watching the endless flow of landing airliners. Generally there are other spectators too – seagulls, starlings, whatever the local flocks consist of – for the environs of an airfield usually spawn a variety of often hazardous bird life.

The differences between the landing 747, with its enormous wing span, tremendous weight and powerful engines, and the birds are obvious. Yet there are many more similarities, and it is the author's belief that mechanical flight's close relationship to natural flight is one of the reasons for its huge appeal to such a wide audience over the entire twentieth cen-

Right: David Hoover leads Cal Howell and Dave Morss in a three-ship formation of Christen Eagle biplanes over the Californian coast. The Eagle is a popular sport aerobatic biplane. (Nicholas Veronico)

Left: The outstanding formation team Red Devils, flying red-painted Pitts biplanes, changed its name to the Eagles in 1979 when it switched to the rainbow-coloured Chisten (Aviat) Eagle aerobatic plane. The Eagles have been a fixture at Oshkosh, and their routine includes this pass, where leader Charlie Hillard rolls inverted while team-mates Tom Poberezny and Gene Soucy, still right side up, follow. (Philip Handleman)

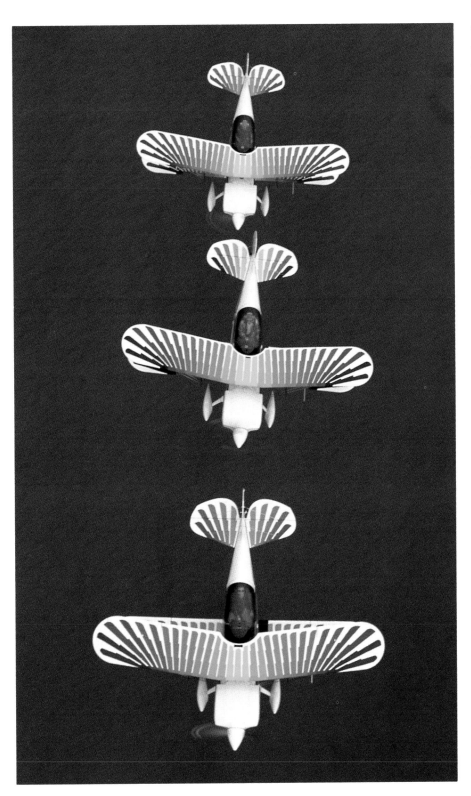

tury. Some primal stirring within us attracts us to things that fly, makes us want to fly ourselves – an inherent wish that extends to the dreams of free flight that almost everyone has experienced.

Some of the similarities between birds and planes are also obvious: a sailplane looking for a thermal certainly resembles a soaring hawk, its wing never beating, perhaps seeking the same rising column of air. Some are more subtle, discernible only through close observation or by watching a slow-motion film, as when a duck comes in to land, arching its wings as if it were deploying flaps, dropping its webbed feet to serve as speed brakes and undercarriage, all the while making minute control corrections that calibrate its speed and flight path with perfect accuracy.

The similarities do not stop there. The structure of a flying bird is perfectly analogous to the structure and mechanics of a flying machine, with exquisite care going into the strength and weight of bony material, the placement and size of the muscle tissue to provide power and the carefully measured use of food as fuel. Beyond basic mechanics, some of the most sophisticated inventions like radar or inertial navigation are surpassed in nature: bats use sonic ranging to find their prey and migrating birds have a built-in navigation system that brings them unerringly across thousands of miles.

However, in none of these areas do aircraft yet approach natural flyers in terms of efficiency. Lightweight aircraft structures have evolved, but they do not heal themselves when broken. Aircraft control responses have become extremely rapid, but they still do not approach the instantaneous, immensely complex response of animal flight. Aircraft are manufactured at great cost and in great quantity, but they do not reproduce. And in the most important area of all, aircraft computers do not even approach the brains of flying animals in terms of capability.

Thus it is no real surprise that when man at last achieved powered flight and developed it to the point when competitions could be held, the public was wildly enthusiastic – as it is to this day. Further, the public's positive reaction to flight has grown and changed with circumstances: as the world has changed, so has aviation, and as aviation has changed so has the public's appreciation of it. It is not unfair to say that the growth and sophistication of the public's taste has been reflected in how it has reacted as it too has become increasingly sophisticated over time. In effect, each period of aviation's development has been matched by a corresponding public attitude. In the first years, indeed, until long after the Wright Brothers had flown, the public was sceptical, and rightly so: there had been many pretenders. But the scepticism changed in the following decade to a sense of wonder at this fabulous new sport that let human beings do what the sages had for centuries said was impossible – fly.

Aircraft had in fact matured only slightly from the Wright Flyer when the first international meeting for aeronautics was held in August 1911 at Reims, France. One of the gorgeous posters advertising the *'Grande Semained'Aviation de la Champagne'* ('The Champagne Region's Great Aviation Week') expressed

the very essence of flight for many years, for it depicts a lissom female figure waving up at dashing aviators defying death as they stream out of the golden sunset. The 'fly-in at Reims' was an aristocratic affair, with the plutocracy staying in expensive hotel suites while the hoi-polloi camped out – not unlike the Fly-In at Oshkosh today. The schedule called for a series of competitions to reach the greatest speeds or altitudes, and the premier event was the *Coupe International d'Aviation*, which became known as the Gordon Bennett Cup after its donor, James Gordon Bennett, who also put up a 25,000-franc prize, worth about $5,000 then and perhaps $500,000 in current dollars.

France had gone mad about aircraft. There were seven aerodromes, as airfields were called, around Paris alone. Thirty-

Above: Beechcraft T-34 trainers of the Lima Lima Squadron *typify the quality flying that takes place at today's warbird air shows. (William Jesse)*

Below: The Boeing B-17 bomber is one of the largest warbirds in existence today. It is obviously very expensive to operate, and there are currently less than a dozen examples flying. (William Jesse)

eight aircraft arrived for the meet, as did more than 100,000 visitors. The weather was not good, and this was reflected in the continual crashes, which themselves delighted the crowd. Yet, beneath the promoters' fervour and the exaggerated reporting, there was serious work under way at Reims, on both national and engineering levels. At the national level, each country cheered its favourite, France having the most entrants to cheer for. Glenn Curtiss was the lone American present, and he was the object of special attention, for his growing feud with the Wright Brothers touched a chord with the European competitors, whom the Wrights also regarded as infringers of patents. At the engineering level, a surprisingly wide variety of aircraft were entered. The celebrities of the Channel

Flight, Louis Blériot and Hubert Latham, brought their monoplanes, which were admired by the crowds for their sleek lines and were as yet unsullied by stories of structural failure. Latham's Antoinette drew the most favourable comments, in part a reflection of the pilot's sophisticated personality and in part because he dared to fly it in 'storm conditions', that is, in winds up to 18mph. Henri Farman flew his large biplane with brilliance, showing off its combination of Wright-like agility and Voisin-like stability. Louis Paulhan's Voisin was essentially a copy of the Wright machine, with a Hargrave-style, box-kite tail which contributed more to drag than to stability.

Reims was to do what many later meets would do – point the way to the future. The Wrights had somewhat pris-

sily declined the invitation of the Aero Club of America to represent the United States at Reims, saying that they were more interested in selling aeroplanes. Curtiss was asked in their place – only one year after he had flown his aircraft. Yet, when the meet was over, two new stars had emerged, Henri Farman, who had set a new world long-distance record of 180 kilometres, and Curtiss, who had blazed around the course in his clipped-wing *Golden Flyer* at 47mph, beating Blériot by a mere six seconds and winning the Gordon Bennett Cup. The Wrights may have been interested in selling aeroplanes, but Curtiss obtained a million dollars' worth of publicity by his win.

Every air show since, whether it be Paris or Farnborough, Oshkosh or Singapore, Vancouver or Moscow, has been a direct descendant of the Reims meet and has incorporated the same people-pleasing qualities – new aircraft, fascinating personalities, the element of danger and the vicarious pleasure of associating with that most agreeable of celebrities, the pilot. But the producers of air shows have grown increasingly aware of the public's needs and tastes and have moulded their preparations to them. When the wonderful week at Reims had ended and the thousands of exhilarated visitors had gone home, everyone was happy because aviation had been advanced – and the promoters had made money. Air shows had a future if they could turn in a profit, and there were promoters and flyers in every country who would cater for the growing desire of the public to see aircraft and their heroic pilots perform.

Within the next sixty days air shows were held in Belgium, Italy, France, Germany and Britain, where, at the Doncaster meet, Hélène Dutrieu demonstrated her pluck by being nonchalant about crashing a Demoiselle. Everywhere flying was embraced by the public, rich or poor, young or old, man or woman. Pilots, conscious of their newly gained star quality, tried to outdo themselves, as Louis Paulhan did in a sterling demonstration at Weybridge, at the Brooklands automobile racetrack. Paulhan's show was so favourably received that it changed the direction of the track's history, converting it for many years into a centre of British aviation experimentation. There was competition both for prizes and for glory, and the effect upon air meets was dramatic. It was no longer sufficient just to be able to fly: now the pilots had to fly faster, higher and farther than their rivals, from one meet to the next. Bigger engines were sought, wings were clipped and greater risks were taken, all in pursuit of better performance.

The first American international aviation meet was held in Los Angeles during the period 10–20 January 1910, at Dominquez Ranch south of the city, with a colossal purse of $80,000 that attracted 58 entrants and 500,000 spectators. The field included current and future luminaries like Charles Willard, Charles Hamilton, Glenn Curtiss, Tom Baldwin, Lincoln Beachey (still flying an airship), Louis Paulhan and Didier Masson (who would wage war in the Mexican skies long before he entered the Lafayette Escadrille). No one knew in 1910 whether the airship or the aeroplane would be the

Right, upper: Admirers at the 1993 Oshkosh Fly-In gather round the immaculate Curtiss P-6E Hawk replica that took owner Ralph Rosanik nearly a lifetime to transform from concept to public display. The Hawk biplanes were snappy little fighters that represented the United States' first line of defence during part of the inter-war period. This series of aircraft culminated in the monoplane Curtiss P-40 that was produced in great numbers for combat in the Second World War. The Rosanik Hawk was kindly loaned to the Experimental Aircraft Association's Air Adventure Museum for the 1993/94 winter. (Philip Handleman)
Right, lower: Here demonstrating its folding wings, the Curtiss Helldiver was a major player in the Pacific War and is worthy of this immaculate restoration. (William Jesse)

dominant vehicle of the future, and Beachey raced his 5,000 cubic foot dirigible against the more experienced Roy Knabenshue. Beachey became friends with Curtiss, who taught him to fly and launched him on a brief but meteoric flying career.

The clear favourite of the crowd was Paulhan in his Farman, who set a world altitude record of 4,165 feet and bested Hamilton in an impromptu race – and had a delightful accent. Yet it was racing which would lead the way in future air shows, for, as much as the public enjoyed the spectacle, it *loved* the speed. By their very nature, attempts at altitude and distance records were remote, but a speed race – ah, that was right in front of the spectators, the engines snarling, the smoke being blown back. And if anything happened, that was right in front of the spectators too. Not that anyone wanted anything to happen, no more than do the spectators at Reno today: they just don't want to miss it if it does!

It was at this time that the world's love affair with flight was drawn to four interacting arenas – racing, record-setting, flights of exploration and, as the most important subset of these, personalities. Only later would all of these combine with the fruits of military aviation development to create a worldwide network of passenger transportation, and with it a totally different popular appreciation of aviation – and one that has generated a need to return to its roots and accounts for the incredible popularity of today's fly-ins.

Racing was the first and perhaps the most enduring of these arenas, for two elements now influenced the rapid advance in speed. Engines became more powerful and, as they did, designers began to, recognize the importance of streamlining. Hitherto, drag had simply been an implicit factor in whatever aeroplane had resulted from the designer's efforts; now a conscious attempt was made to slip, rather than force, the aircraft through the air.

Inspiration for much of the change came through the efforts of a man who would become world famous for his Spad fighter designs in the First World War – Louis Bechereau. Working for Armand Deperdussin, Bechereau improved on previous attempts by the Nieuport firm to achieve a truly streamlined aircraft by using a revolutionary new structure, the monocoque fuselage. The streamlined fuselage was made of moulded plywood, which would be seen again during the war in the Albatros fighters and even later in the Lockheed Vega.

The Deperdussin, powered by a whirling, 160-horsepower, fourteen-cylinder Gnome Rhône rotary engine, was the first to break the 100mph barrier. Flown by the tempestuous Jules Védrines at Pau, France, on 12 February 1912, the beautiful little monoplane hurtled round the course at 162.53kph (100.21mph). By September Védrines would raise this to 108.16mph in Chicago, Illinois, and win the Gordon Bennett Cup. He went on to become a hero in the Great War, flying clandestine missions to drop spies behind enemy lines.

The quest for speed was to receive its biggest boost when the great French sportsman Jacques Schneider established

Right, upper: When he is not flying with the Eagles, Gene Soucy is thrilling crowds as the pilot of a modified Grumman Ag Cat called Showcat. Riding atop the aircraft is accomplished wing-walker Teresa Stokes. (Philip Handleman)
Right, lower: Referred to as 'The Great One' by air show announcers, Robert R. A. (Bob) Hoover has been on the air show circuit for as long as anyone can remember. A decorated Army Air Forces combat pilot in the Second World War, he was later a test pilot and a flying chum of Chuck Yeager. For years he has piloted a twin-engine Shrike Commander, performing an 'energy management' series of manoeuvres: making it look simple, he brings the aircraft to a halt at a predetermined spot after shutting down both engines in flight. In April 1993 his medical certificate was revoked by the FAA, but, not one quietly to accept such diktats, he appealed. His effort for reinstatement included a special air show performance with a check pilot aboard, executed expressly for a Federal judge in Oklahoma City. The judge was persuaded, and as of early 1994 Hoover was flying again. Yet on further appeal he was once more grounded, and at the time of writing he was pursuing his case in the courts. (Philip Handleman)

'La Coupe d'Aviation Maritime Jacques Schneider'. For the first time, racing rules were drawn up which would foster the development of commercial aircraft, for the entrants were required to be capable of operating from the open sea, be reliable and possess an adequate range. Rather than individuals, the contest was intended for aero clubs, both to promote their growth and prestige and to prevent the proliferation of amateur entries. Only three aircraft per club were allowed, to keep the number of entrants to a manageable size and to prevent the wealthiest clubs from swamping the smaller. The specifications were laudable but easily converted to the goals of the clubs, which wanted to build small, single-seat speedsters. Like so many pioneers in aviation, Schneider would die before seeing his objective achieved, as it ultimately was, not by Schneider Cup racers but by the beautiful British Empire boats and the Pan American clippers.

Only two Schneider races were run before war broke out in 1914. In the 1913 race stock French monoplanes, the Nieuport, Deperdussin and Morane Saulnier, were fitted with floats. Maurice Prévost flew his 160-horsepower Deperdussin to first place, his average of 45.74mph including the time he had spent on the surface after an incorrect finish. In 1914 the race took on an international flavour, with entrants from Britain, France, Germany, Switzerland and the United States. The British entry, the Sopwith Tabloid, was particularly significant for it recognized the propaganda value in winning the immediately prestigious trophy. The race heralded Great Britain's determina-

tion to reign in the air as she did on the sea.

The First World War interrupted the racing, even as it advanced the technology for the post-war racers. The public's attitude had changed, as it began to realize the potential of this new-born baby, aviation, in both the commercial and the military worlds. Speeds in the Schneider Trophy competition would climb year by year. In recognition of the prestige and influence the race exercised over the development of fighting aircraft, the dictator Benito Mussolini would throw the resources of his country behind the Italian entrants. It would then take the inspirational efforts of Lady Lucy Houston, Supermarine and Rolls-Royce to overcome the Italian challenge, so that Flight

Lieutenant John Boothman could raise the record to 340.08mph in 1931. He secured permanent possession of the Trophy by flying around the course in his 2,300-horsepower Supermarine S.6B.

The immediate effect of such speeds was, however, slight. Fighters were still flying at under 200mph and transports were still bumbling along at 110mph. But the superheated engineering necessary to get the very best airframes and engines improved the breed in Britain, Italy and the United States, and in Germany and France even though the latter two nations never formally competed. The public sensed this, and the more perceptive journalists of the time announced it. To attain the speed it was necessary to obtain more power. To get more power it was necessary to improve metallurgy, lubrication, carburation and fuel and, above all, to improve the cooling of both fuel and water. To handle the speed produced, airframes had to be stronger and more streamlined, propellers had to be more efficient and pilots had to have extra skills. All this progress had direct implications for military and commercial aircraft design.

The sport of air racing had become increasingly popular in America, fostered by the publicity given to the Gordon Bennett and Pulitzer races, which were used by the US military as research and development tools. The two races were, roughly, the land-based equivalents of the Schneider Trophy event, and when the Depression killed off military funding for development, there blossomed forth the National Air Races, begin in 1929 and brought to full bloom by Cliff Henderson, the great race promoter who truly understood the public's love affair with the phenomenon of flight.

In many ways Henderson performed a miracle. While aviation was popular in the United States, the relatively infrequent air races did not have stature, but Henderson orchestrated the National Air Races in such a way that they conferred both standing and legitimacy upon the participants, becoming, as it were, a World Series of air racing. A company that built the engine that won the Bendix or Thompson Trophies received not only publicity but orders. For a young pilot the races were a ticket to the big time: a win or even a good finish in the Cleveland Races made his name a household word. By 1932 the unthinkable had happened:

headlines featured Jimmy Doolittle and his Gee Bee rather than the baseball pennant races. The National Air Races came to be an expression of an increasing expectation among the aviation public that a commercial basis for flying was beginning to emerge, that all of the thousands of millions poured into aviation by government and private citizens would begin at last to pay a return beyond subsidized mail and passenger services.

Yet, to succeed, the National Air Races had to have all the glitter of Hollywood, the romance of the visiting celebrities and the raw power of the Indianapolis 500. Henderson juggled a dozen balls in the air, keeping temperamental race pilots in line, making sure that reporters got their stories, working with manufacturers to provide prizes, inviting new acts to delight the crowds and always having plenty of pretty girls on hand. Something was happening every minute: if the races themselves weren't on, then there would be military fly-overs, aerobatic teams, parachutists or an intriguing juxtaposition like an autogiro 'dogfighting' with a Curtiss Pusher.

At Cleveland, Henderson was careful to maintain a variety of races, from those limited to small-displacement engines up to the unlimited Thompson and Bendix. Pilots and manufacturers could 'trade up' as they gained experience. The beauty of Henderson's spectacle was that it was open to anyone with the brains and the courage to create a competitive aeroplane. All over the country men with talent if not engineering degrees produced racers with tiny wings and big engines. Their names are now legendary – Steve

Wittman with his *Buster* and his *Bonzo*; Jimmy Wedell with his stable of aesthetically pleasing, intuitively designed racers, perhaps the greatest of the era; the five Granville brothers with their much maligned Gee Bees, now given full respectability with Darryl Benjamin's impeccable flight routines in the reproduction R-2; Clayton Folkerts and his tiny speedsters; and Benny Howard, with an eye on commerce as well as speed. Most of the aircraft were crowd-pleasers, as were most of the pilots, men like Jimmy Doolittle, Roscoe Turner, Art Chester and Rudy Kling. One pilot was not well received, for chauvinistic reasons: Michael Detroyat brought his sleek little blue Caudron C.460 to Cleveland and beat his American competitors in both the Greve and the Thompson races in 1936, adding insult to injury by requiring only 370 horsepower from his Renault Bengali engine to do so.

Unforgivable! – and also a commentary on the times, and on the fact that nations evolved air racing to suit national temperaments. Thus the French enjoyed the *Coupe Deutsch* races, their elegant airframes making the most of a limited number of cubic centimetres, while the British preferred the gentler, sportsman-like nature of the King's Cup races, where a complicated system of handicaps opened the field to many. These races, however, occasionally spawned more robust contests like the 1936 Schlesinger England to South Africa Race, where hot little planes like the Percival Mew Gull suddenly developed from a staid touring plane background.

It was primarily in America that racing advanced the state of the art, pushing engines, propellers and drag-reduction to new levels. It was also an age when winning a race could propel an unknown mechanic from an anonymous garage to

Left: Resplendent in Navy colours and markings, this Grumman Avenger is truly a classic warbird. (William Jesse)

headlines and the full-time manufacture of aircraft. And, sadly, it was an age when the requirements for flying skill and aircraft integrity were not rigorous, and there were many casualties.

The Second World War brought unprecedented advances in aviation, even as the great mass of people turned to air power as the panacea to end this war and prevent the next one. It also brought to an end the era of home-built racers. When racing returned in 1946, it was in surplus military aircraft. For some the sport was never the same; for others it was even more thrilling. Bill Odum's tragic crash in the beautiful *Beguine* put an end to racing at Cleveland, though it began again in earnest at Reno in 1964 and has grown steadily more popular ever since. The incredible thing is that, in a country where bass fishing occupies several hours of television air time a week, the Reno Air Races are ignored by the media.

The urge to set records must be something inherent in humanity, for, from the first air meet to the present day, a record in any form has existed only for someone else to break. In the early years it was relatively easy: ordinary progress enabled pilots to lift speed, altitude, endurance, distance and flights from point to point on a recurring basis. But, in relatively short order, record-breaking aircraft came to be tailored for specific tasks, and hence both more expensive and more difficult to fly. As dashing as the Deperdussin was when Védrines first passed the 100mph mark, most of his contemporaries could have flown it. The same could not be said of the malicious handful that was the Messerschmitt Bf 109R in which Fritz Wendel set the world speed record in 1939, or the modified Second World War P-51 Mustang *Dago Red* in which the late Frank Taylor set a speed record of 517.1mph.

Right: The Grumman F6F Hellcat was one of the architects of American domination during the Pacific War. Restoring this F6F-5N in California took over three years – with superb results. (William Jesse)

Fly Past, Fly Present

In the heyday of absolute piston-engine speed records, it was customary for first one nation and then another to excel, the progress marking the relative status of that country's next generation of fighter aircraft. Thus, in a eight-year period from 1923 to 1931, the absolute speed record was set eight times by four nations, the United States, France, Italy and Great Britain. In that interval speeds rose from the 233.00mph achieved by the inimitable Sadi Lecointe flying a svelte Nieuport 29 to the blistering 406.94mph reached by Flight Lieutenant G. H. Stainforth in a Supermarine S.6B. Italy then took over, Lieutenant Francesco Agello flying the gorgeous (and still extant) Macchi Castoldi MC.72 to 440.60mph at Lago di Garda – a record that still stands.

Altitude records did not hold quite the interest for the public that speed dashes did, but governments were interested in them because of their relevance to the development of aeronautical engineering and combat performance. The progress was steady if considerably more sedate. The first record was Hubert Latham's 508 feet in an Antoinette in August 1909; by 1915 it had been raised to 20,079 feet by Georges Legagneux in a Nieuport.

One of the differences between altitude and speed records was the question of physics: a man could travel extremely fast without needing an oxygen mask, but pilots soon found that above 18,000 feet oxygen was a necessity. The last official piston-engine altitude record was set by Lieutenant Mario Pezzi in an open-cockpit Caproni 161*bis* biplane. He wore a pressure suit that looked as though it were derived from diver's outfit and his aeroplane featured a huge propeller, high-aspect wings and very light construction. With the advent of the jet engine and pressurized cabins, altitude records lit-

Right: The Santa Monica Museum of Flying has a P-51 which races each year at the National Championship Air Races at Reno, Nevada. This the much modified Dago Red. *(Nicholas Veronico)*

Left: The Museum of Flying has added a second cockpit to the P-51D Miss America. Dual instruction is available in this hot Second World War fighter. (Nicholas Veronico)

erally went through the roof, the Space Shuttle taking them to a height in orbit of 356.46 miles.

A more enduring element of record-setting, and one which struck a chord with more people, was the first flight between two points. The London *Daily Mail* did its best to encourage these, and, having induced Paulhan to win the London to Manchester race in 1910 and Blériot to cross the English Channel in 1911, it next sought to advance aviation (and increase its circulation) with a crossing of the Atlantic. This was illuminated by Harry Hawker's dramatic forced landing and delayed notice of rescue and by the courage of Alcock and Brown, shepherding

their Vickers Vimy through cloud and ice from Newfoundland to Ireland. (Circumstances change, things progress, but the courage of flyers remains constant: even as these words are being written, a Vickers Vimy replica is being built to recreate that flight, and then, with a suitable change of colour and detail, to recreate another epic Vimy flight, that of the brothers Ross and Keith Smith, who flew from London to Australia in 1920, blazing a trail over terrible terrain until they finally reached their destination and went on to make a triumphal cross-continent tour.)

The record flights captured the essence of the phenomenon of aviation, that of pitting human endeavour against seemingly impossible odds. They also underlined a new era of public expectation – the commercial exploitation of aviation, which, however, would not be brought to fruition until the 1950s. Yet the growth of post-war commercial aviation had its genesis in the early days of record flights. Then national honour was involved, and every country with the necessary resources attempted to participate, especially when there was an inducement like the Orteig Prize, $25,000 for the first flight between New York and Paris. The monetary value of the prize, while considerable for the time, was secondary to the national and individual prestige its winning would confer.

In many countries pilots and designers combined to push the leading edge of aviation farther into the future. Thus in the late 1920s there were Charles Nungesser and François Coli in their *White Bird*, anxious to win for France, while on the other side of the ocean Nungesser's wartime colleague Réné Fonck was preparing to fly a Sikorsky biplane. From the Netherlands, his wartime manufacturing activities for Germany still not forgotten, came Tony Fokker to prepare one of his trimotor F.VIIs, *America*, for the famous explorer Richard Byrd. Charles Levine, a man castigated for almost inadvertently introducing a commercial tinge to aviation, was backing Italian-born Giuseppe Bellanca's marvellous *Columbia* for a series of pilots before settling on Clarence Chamberlin. Then, from out of the West, came the spoiler, a young man who set the aviation world alight with a spectacular solo flight to win the Orteig Prize in a Ryan NYP, *Spirit of St Louis*. Lindbergh became the most acclaimed individual of his time, aviation's ambassador to the world.

The country and the world went aviation crazy, a phenomenon that happened to coincide with the advent of reliable air-cooled radial engines and a frisky stock market where investors wanted to get in on the ground floor of the next major industry. For the next ten years there was a plethora of record flights from all countries, and great names emerged: Bert Hinckler, for his solo flight to Australia; Lady Heath, the first woman to fly from South Africa to England; France's Dieudonne Costes and Lieutenant-Commander Le Brix in their commemorative Breguet XIX *Nungesser-Coli*, flying nonstop across the South Atlantic; Germany's trio in the Junkers W.33 *Bremen*, making the first east–west crossing of the Atlantic; and the immortal Charles Kingsford-Smith and C. T. P. Ulm in their Fokker VIIB *Southern Cross*, making the first true trans-Pacific flight.

With each flight the crowds assembled to wish the flyers well on take-off and watch the long, rumbling roll as the overladen planes struggled into the air. At the destination point other crowds were waiting, along with reporters, local dignitaries and assurances of lasting fame. Occasionally the crowds waited in vain, as they had to do for Nungesser and Coli, and later for too many of the Dole Race contestants. Malevolent fate seemed to toy with some of the heroes, ladling out success after success before exacting the toll. Kingsford-Smith barely savoured his

Right: For many years the world's warbirds capital was Harlingen in Texas, the Confederate Air Force – the leading organization dedicated to the preservation of Second World War aircraft – being based at nearby Rebel Field. However, the burgeoning collection and the growing crowds at the spectacular CAF annual show in early October forced a move by the groups's headquarters to Midland in the early 1990s. The typical midday cumulus clouds of the Gulf coast form a delightful backdrop for this SNJ, the US Navy version of the AT-6, at Harlingen in 1989. (Philip Handleman)

triumphs before he was lost in his beautiful *Lady Southern Cross*; Amelia Earhart pushed her quest for records beyond her capabilities in her round-the-world attempt; Wiley Post, a veteran of epic round-the-world flights himself, crashed to his death in a hybrid lash-up of an aeroplane in a capricious accident that took Will Rogers with him. Yet the tragedies were part of the phenomenon of flight as well, exactly defining the currency with which progress was being purchased.

The capacity to please the public with record flights has not died. Dick Rutan and Jeana Yeager kept an unbelieving world glued to its television sets for nine days as they fought their recalcitrant *Voyager* around the globe, non-stop and unrefuelled, in 1986. They let everyone know that there are still records to be set and places to be explored.

At first, aircraft were seen as an extension of the explorer's toolbox, a new means to reach uncharted lands. The public responded eagerly to the concept of aircraft probing the North and South Poles, and Rear-Admiral Richard Byrd was determined to be the first to the North,

after unsuccessful attempts by rivals George Hubert Wilkins, Roald Amundsen and Lincoln Ellsworth. Byrd, with pilot Floyd Bennett, took the Fokker F.VIIa-3m *Josephine Ford* over the Pole on 9 May 1926; and on 28/29 November he and pilot Bernt Balchen took the Ford Trimotor over the South Pole in a flight that has been the subject of controversy over the years.

The Arctic was the route preferred by Soviet pilots to demonstrate the incredible range of their ANT-25 aircraft. Three Heroes of the Soviet Union, Valery P. Chkalov, Georgi F. Baidukov and Alexander V. Belyakov, flew 5,288 miles from Moscow to Vancouver, Canada, on 18–20 June 1937. A month later, on 12–14 July, a second trans-polar crew composed of the Soviet Union's premier pilot, Mikhail Gromov, with Andrei B. Yumashyev and Sergei A. Danilin, flew the long-wingspan ANT-25 monoplane to San Jacinto, California – 6,036 miles in 62 hours 17 minutes, a new world record.

The advent of reliable amphibians like the Sikorsky series opened up the wilds of Africa to explorers like Osa and Martin Johnson, who entertained the world with films brought back from 'The Dark Continent'. But, unlike the great adventuring days of sail, when explorers like Columbus and Magellan sought new countries where new wealth could be exploited, aviation's greatest efforts of exploration lay in expanding the regime of flight, examining new phenomena. The frontiers that were pushed back were not those of countries or continents: they were instead those of science and then of commerce. All over the world, aircraft were designed to expand the envelope of science with investigations into flutter, stability, weather, icing, instrumentation, navigation, pressurization and, in 1947, the sonic barrier. When two young lieutenants, Lester Maitland and Albert Hegenberger, flew their *Bird of Paradise* to Hawaii they were not trying to rediscover the island but rather to demonstrate foolproof means of navigating to it quickly and accurately. When Jimmy Doolittle flew his little Consolidated Husky entirely on instruments, he was exploring a path that has led directly to today's 'glass cockpits'. Howard Hughes was making a commercial statement in his round-the-world flight, just as Hanna Reitsch was in her Focke-Achgelis helicopter.

As aircraft improved, it became obvious that the exploration of new flight regimes was worth pursuing only if it led to practical – that is, commercial – results. A perfect example can be found in the 1934 London to Australia race, won by the purposeful De Havilland DH 88 Comet, of which both an original example and a beautiful reproduction are flying today. But the Comet was a racing plane pure and simple: it won the race and led to nothing but a body of knowledge that was useful in the later De Havilland Mosquito. In contrast, the second- and third-placed aircraft, the KLM Douglas DC-2 and the Boeing 247D, served notice to the world that it was on the threshold of abundant international airline travel.

Almost from aviation's very beginning, great personalities have come forward, advancing their cause as much by charm as by their flying skills. Everyone

Right: *The Collings Foundation's B-24 and B-17 in formation over California's Sonoma Valley. (Nicholas Veronico)*

has favourites whose names leap immediately to mind: Roscoe Turner, resplendent in his uniform; Doolittle, quiet, succinct, his reserve blessed by a tremendous smile; Earhart, who managed to be demure and aggressive at the same time; the Mollisons, who singly and together made aviation history; Douglas Bader, so proud and, surprisingly, so amusing; Stanford-Tuck, with whom Bader developed a wonderful cross-talk relationship; Ernst Udet, in his element as a showman and an aerobatic pilot; Italo Balbo, intelligent and flamboyant; Howard Hughes, who could be personable at the end of a

record flight if rarely at other times; Bevo Howard, an irrepressible showman; Bob Hoover, the gentle professional; Harald Penrose, an intuitive test pilot and marvellous aviation historian; Anne Lindbergh, competent crew member for her husband and a lyrical writer. There were hundreds more, in every country.

Equally important are those within industry, whose towering personalities spurred advances whatever the commercial climate. Just as every country was able to produce outstanding aeroplanes, so were they also able to produce great designers and manufacturers. The names

Above: A Dassault Super Etendard, not yet retired from world service but 'preserved' by dint of an air show. (Tim Laming)

are a roll call of honour: Sopwith, De Havilland, Handley Page, Curtiss, Boeing, Potez, Bloch, Martin, Douglas, Northrop, Messerschmitt, Tupolev – the list goes on and on. But there were others as well, whose names are less well known outside the industry but revered within it: Johnson, Rich, Barnwell, Folland, Horten, Berlin, Hall, Mitchell, Laddon, Günther, Tank – far too many to name, each one the author of a classic aircraft hallowed today.

Each of these, and the greater numbers they represent, realized that there was a huge barrier holding back aviation – profitability. The industry had for years been subsidized, either by governments or by investors who wryly advised newcomers that there was a lot of money in aviation because they had left all theirs in it. The Second World War accelerated the breaking of that barrier, but it must be remembered that every significant advance in aviation that appeared during the war had its origins in the pioneering test work carried out in the preceding years. All the great advances – more powerful engines, jet engines, superchargers, pressurization, reversible propellers, radar, loran – had been initiated before the war, sometimes as much as two decades before.

After 1945, as the great four-engine transports began to ply the world's airways, it seemed as though the days of profitable aviation were at hand. The image was enhanced by a sudden boom in the production of light planes; indeed, for the first two years after the war it seemed as though aircraft were going to follow the path of the automobile. But even as

light plane production fell back, commercial aviation thrived. The De Havilland Comet made its awesome debut, only to become a victim of inadequate engineering requirements. When the Boeing 707 came along there were many who said that it would follow the career of the Comet: it was too fast, too complex and too expensive to operate. But it confounded the critics and the jet age in international travel dawned.

And with it came a change in the public's outlook. As the jets proliferated and as business travel became routine, flying was no longer a glamorous treat, something to save up for and write home about. Instead it became more and more of a chore. Aircraft grew larger, flight attendants became too overloaded with work to cosset the passenger, terminals spread out and became more difficult to penetrate and the linear programming geniuses developed the idea of the hub system to increase passenger load factors. The public, quite reasonably, became jaded, now regarding what had once been an intoxicating experience as little more than a bus ride.

Amazingly, this manifold expansion in flying was achieved, at least in the West, with a continually improving safety record. When accidents did occur, they garnered more attention because the loss of life was greater. However, the cold statistics were understood: you were far safer flying in a commercial airliner than you were in any other mode of transport. This understanding no doubt accounts in part for the fact that the number of passenger-miles continues to grow, and is forecast to do so for the next decade.

Fly Past, Fly Present

But while the bloom may be off the rose in terms of the personal enjoyment of commercial air travel, the public's enthusiasm for the phenomenon of flight is growing in other areas. There has in fact been, especially in the United States, a healthy transference from the passive appreciation of aviation as something to admire, but not participate in personally, to a much more involved, 'hands-on' approach. Much of the transference stems from the activities of the Experimental Aviation Association, an organization that grew from a few 'buffs' meeting in Paul Poberezny's basement to an international organization that has an enormous influence on aviation legislation as well as aviation development.

The most obvious manifestation of the EAA's importance is of course the annual Fly-In at Oshkosh, the premier attraction in aviation today, with hundreds of thousands of people and thousands of aircraft of every type in attendance. There is an almost mystic quality about Oshkosh. It is one of the most egalitarian events in the world, where one will see doctors, lawyers, politicians and film stars sitting quietly in a symposium, listening to a garage mechanic from Pennsylvania instruct them in one of the arcane arts of home-building. It is also one of the best-humoured and most courteous events, where people troop in line to admire the classics, the warbirds and the home-builts, coming close enough to touch but refraining from doing so.

There is no question that the EAA has saved a moribund general aviation industry in the United States and, in the

Right: Although the De Havilland Dove might not be regarded as a particularly exciting aircraft, this Royal Jordanian Air Force example – an exceptionally rare visitor to Britain – was one of the most popular exhibits at the 1993 International Air Tattoo. (Tim Laming)

ROYAL JORDANIAN AIR FORCE سلاح الجو الملكي الأردني

JY-RJU

Left: Even air show celebrities like the world famous Red Arrows *face an uncertain future in the cost-conscious 1990s. (Tim Laming)*

process, totally revised its own approach to aviation. When the EAA began, it did not pretend to advance the state of the art; instead, the emphasis was simply on constructing light aircraft, often modelling them on the home-builts of the past, or on the creation of hybrids using components from several aeroplanes – a cut-down Cub fuselage, the wings from a T-craft. Now, the home-builders of the EAA are not only advancing the state of the art, they are paving the way for industry, demonstrating new techniques, new aerofoils, new engines. If someone had predicted in 1955 that the great Beech Aircraft Company would one day build a corporate aircraft based on principles developed in the home-built industry, the speaker would have been an object of ridicule. No one could have believed that a whole host

of new engines would emerge to power an entirely new type of ultra-light aircraft, and that some of the latter would become certified for production by the Federal Aviation Administration. Each year has brought something new, from home-built helicopters to Jim Bede's home-built BD-10 executive jet.

A complementary movement, not so formally organized, has grown up in parallel with the EAA – the worldwide interest in restoration. In every country, even those struggling to emerge from the wreckage of the Soviet Union, craftsmen are restoring aircraft to 'as new' or better standards. What was once the preserve of the museums has now grown to mammoth proportions, with no project too complex to undertake. The restoration movement has also spawned some indus-

Fly Past, Fly Present

tries, again not so formally organized as those building ultra-lights or kits, but influential none the less. These are the individuals and companies that gather the parts and materials for restorations, who reproduce the fabric, the tyres, the turnbuckles and wires no longer generally available in the market place.

So in many ways the phenomenon of flight has come full circle: the public's appreciation for flying has grown, surviving the inevitable disillusionment of modern jet travel to focus on the exciting aspects of the modern home-built and restoration movements. Curiously enough, while the tendency in many pastimes, like sport, is for passive participation, watching the game on television, aviation is experiencing a resurgence of active involvement. The crowds at Reims may have enjoyed the planes and the

Left: An impossible sight in the West but a few years ago: the mighty Tu-95 'Bear'. (Tim Laming)
Right: *The* Patrouille Suisse *display team operates the Hawker Hunter, a classic aircraft still in service decades after its first flight. (Tim Laming)*

Left: A superbly restored North American F-86 Sabre trails its distinctive plume of brown smoke. (Tim Laming)

pilots, but they would have understood little of what was taking place. The crowds at Oshkosh still enjoy the planes and the pilots, but they have a tremendous knowledge of what is happening. New developments are eagerly followed: if a Long-eze flies one year, one can be sure that there will be half a dozen variants on the theme the next.

Finally, if there is any doubt that the phenomenon of flight is alive and well, one only has to look at the calendar of events in the world's flying magazines: there are more activities taking place in any one month than there were in twelve just a few years ago. The most popular shows on cable television concern flying; aviation magazines are now better than ever; and where once there were perhaps a hundred aviation books published in a year, there are now thousands. A similar

spurt in interest has seen aircraft modelling grow from a child's hobby of rubber-powered, stick-and-paper creations to radio-controlled reproductions so convincing that they can be used in the making of commercial films.

It is true that increased regulation and rising costs have caused problems, but these are more than offset by the availability of professional associations as advocates and by an increase in the number of options open to pilots. One can now buy or hire an aircraft, join a flying club or go into partnership with two, five or ten others. The increase in accessibility represented by air shows, flying clubs and the media has spurred a new interest in flying, and the phenomenon of flight is no longer confined to admiration for heroes. It is out there, waiting to involve anyone who is interested.

Preserving the Heritage

Bob Ogden/William Jesse

The first successful balloon ascent took place in France in 1783 and gliding pioneers were flying at the end of the nineteenth century. In November 1906 the Brazilian Alberto Santos-Dumont made a sustained flight of over 700 feet in France. Prior to these feats many had tried to fly, attempts being made to design aerial machines of differing concepts. The continent of Europe was at the forefront in the development of flying, and it is appropriate that the successes be recorded in museums and collections. In the latter part of the nineteenth century a number of cities became locations for technical museums, and those in Budapest, London, Munich, Prague and Vienna were soon to add aeronautical items to their displays. A number of early aviators donated their aircraft to these museums and, fortunately, most of the machines survive today.

The Kozlekedesi Muzeum in Budapest was established in 1896 and an aeronautical section was soon added. Two early aircraft, the 1910 Zselyi-Aladar 2 and the 1911 Horvath 2 or 3, were placed on show along with engines and compo-

nents. Sadly, the museum was bombed during the Second World War and the two aircraft were lost. Only the engine of the Zselyi-Aladar survived, and this is now fitted to a faithful replica which was constructed for the reopening of the collection in 1966. A new aviation section was set up in an adjacent building in the mid-1980s and this houses a selection of indigenous powered aircraft and gliders

The impressive Technisches Museum für Industrie und Gerwerbe in Vienna opened in 1918 and added an aviation section nine years later. The oldest exhibit is an 1894 glider built and flown by the German pioneer Otto Lilienthal, while the second Taube monoplane built by Igo Etrich in 1910 is another prized item. A major refurbishment of the museum is now taking place and the reopening is planned for 1996. The Narodni Technical Muzeum in Prague is one of the oldest in Europe and its origins go back to 1799. The museum opened in the Schwarzenburg Palace in 1908 and included a fairly large aeronautical display. A new building was ready in 1941 but the exhibits were not moved in until 1945.

Below: The Fokker D.VII was one of the outstanding aircraft of the First World War. This example was flown in a number of Hollywood films. In 1981 the Fokker company bought the biplane at an auction and after restoration it was loaned to the Militaire Luchtvaart Museum at Kamp van Zeist near Utrecht. (Bob Ogden)

Oskar von Miller founded the Deutsches Museum in Munich in 1903 but it was not until 1925 that the first exhibition hall was opened. Eighty per cent of the museum and its contents were destroyed in 1944–45 and many significant aircraft were lost. However, reconstruction commenced in 1948 and the initial aeronautical display was housed in its original area, rebuilt as accurately as possible to its pre-war form. Several early aircraft which had escaped total destruc-

tion in the bombing raids were rebuilt and put on show: these included a Rumpler Taube which had been presented to the museum in 1911, a Grade A donated by the designer in 1917 and the only genuine surviving Wright A. A new hall was added in 1984 and this more than doubled the number of aircraft on view. The new section houses several German designs from the inter-war period.

Over the years the collection had grown steadily and even with the new

hall less than half the exhibits could be placed on show. The museum had a store at the historic airfield of Oberschleissheim, north of the city. In continuous use since it was set up over eighty years ago by the Royal Bavarian Flying Corps, it included many original buildings. The museum refurbished hangars and workshops constructed between 1912 and 1919 and added to them a modern exhibition hall. This superb display opened in September 1992 and has been steadily improved since then.

The 1851 Great Exhibition in London led to the formation of the South Kensington Museum which opened in 1857, and rapid industrial and scientific develop-

ments resulted in the Science Museum's becoming a separate entity in 1901. In 1896 Sir Hiram Maxim donated a model of, and components from, his gigantic but unsuccessful flying machine. The collection includes A. V. Roe's original triplane in which, on 13 July 1909, he made the first real flight in an all-British aeroplane. For several years the museum had the original Wright Flyer on view, but this was returned to the United States after the Second World War. During the conflict the aircraft exhibits were stored and at the end of hostilities they were put on temporary exhibition. A new gallery designed to represent a hangar was opened in 1963 with the transatlantic Vickers

Above: The famous German designer Kurt Tank was responsible for many Focke Wulf types during the Second World War and in the 1950s and 1960s headed the team at Hindustan Aircraft in India. The Marut jet first flew in 1960 and entered production seven years later. This example was presented by India to the Deutsches Museum and is pictured a few days before the opening of the latter's Schleissheim facility in September 1992. (Bob Ogden)

Vimy flown by Alcock and Brown in 1919 as the centrepiece. Among other significant aircraft on show are Amy Johnson's Gipsy Moth, which she flew solo from England to Australia in 1930; the Supermarine S.6B which won the last Schneider Trophy race in 1931; and the Gloster E.28/39, which was the first jet to fly in Britain when it took to the air in May 1941. Restricted space, a problem with most museums, has led to the acquisition of hangars at Wroughton near Swindon and here a number of interesting airliners are based.

Smaller collections in other cities such as Oslo, Stockholm and Helsingør have important aircraft on show. All of these collections are of the 'old school' of European technical museums but have added modern, innovative displays where appropriate.

The first purely aeronautical museum to be formed was the Musée de l'Air in France. Général Caquot, an engineer, collected many items and placed them in store at Issy. An building constructed in 1878 for the Paris Exhibition had been moved to Chalais-Meudon to serve as a hangar for the airship *La France*, and the museum was officially opened in this structure in November 1921. The site proved to be inconvenient for visitors so a new building was constructed in the Boulevard Victor and several aircraft were placed on show there from 1936. These halls were damaged in 1940 and the collection was returned to Meudon, but after a limited amount of restoration the museum opened again in 1950. The building was sited in a research establishment and I well remember my first visit there in 1956. Aircraft mainly from the pre-Second World War days were everywhere – parked on the floor, mounted on pedestals and suspended from the ceiling. Cabinets containing smaller items were filling every gap. On a second visit three years later I was taken to another hangar where more aircraft, engines and components were crammed into the vast building.

The 1970s saw a move to Le Bourget airfield, north of Paris. Opened during the First World War, this was the major airport for the city until Orly became active in the 1950s. In 1951 the *Salon de l'Aéronautique* moved to Le Bourget, where exhibition halls were erected. The construction of the new Charles de Gaulle Airport at Roissy meant that hangars would be vacated and the Director of the museum, Général Pierre Lissarague, was quick to take advantage of the situation, moving aircraft in from Meudon and other storage sites. The first hall opened in 1975 and by 1981 five were finished, showing more than 150 aircraft. The display at Meudon was reorganized to cover the pre-1918 period, but when a terminal building became available this was modified and the early aircraft were transferred to it. This area now has the best collection of aircraft from this era anywhere in the world. Along with all the halls, the displays are presented with flair, and it is a

pity that so few visitors come to the exhibition. The museum suffered a major disaster in 1990 when a fire in a storage hangar at Dugny, on the other side of Le Bourget, destroyed over forty aircraft, including several irreplaceable machines. A purpose-built complex of stores and workshops has recently been completed here.

The use of aircraft by the military during the First World War led to the idea of museums devoted to the history and traditions of the services. In 1917 Lord Rothermere, Secretary of State for Air, persuaded the Air Council to decree that one example of every First World War aircraft type be saved. The Royal Air Force came into being on 1 April 1918 and it was also the intention to preserve one of every type used. Sadly, apart from an exhibition at the National Agricultural Hall in

Above: This Sopwith Camel, built by Boulton and Paul, flew for just over two hours before being sold to a civilian owner in 1923. Acquired by R. G. K. Nash in 1935, it was, with the rest of his historic aircraft, sold to the Royal Aeronautical Society and has been at the RAF Museum since it opened. (Bob Ogden)
Right: In 1946 this Saab B-18 force-landed on the frozen sea off Sundsvall. The wreck was raised in 1979 and the manufacturers and the Swedish Air Force commenced restoration. The aircraft was ready for the opening of the second phase of the Flygvapenmuseum at Malmslatt near Linkoping in 1989. (Bob Ogden)

Islington, little was done, although a few aircraft went to the Imperial War Museum and others to the Science Museum. The idea was revived in the early 1960s when John Tanner, who was on the staff of the Royal Air Force College at Cranwell, published a paper. In 1962 the Air Force Board established a committee and eventually recommended that a museum be set up with Dr Tanner as Director. Just prior to this an officer at RAF Bicester had ordered the scrapping of a Handley Page Hampden and a Dornier Do 17.

The site chosen was the RAF station at Hendon, which had been used by the military since 1914. In the inter-war period great crowds would flock to see the RAF pageants, but urban development caused all powered flying to cease in 1957.

Two of the early hangars were converted into exhibition halls and new additions, including the imposing entrance area, were built. The display was opened by HM Queen Elizabeth II in November 1972. Since that date two new exhibition areas have been added: the Battle of Britain Hall was ready in November 1978 and the Bomber Command Museum followed in April 1983. The exhibitions, which are constantly being improved, present an informative history of the service and over eighty aircraft are on show.

Although a historic site, Hendon suffers from not being an active airfield and new exhibits have to be transported in by road at enormous cost. The Museum maintains workshops and stores at Cardington in Bedfordshire and also administers the

Fly Past, Fly Present

Aerospace Museum at RAF Cosford near Wolverhampton, where more than sixty types are on show and some additions can be flown in. Cosford also houses a number of airliners donated by British Airways.

The other service museums are situated on active airfields, and both the Fleet Air Arm Museum at Yeovilton and the Museum of Army Flying have developed considerably. The display at Yeovilton had humble beginnings as it started with three historic aircraft parked close to a viewing area. The museum opened in 1964, and during the 1970s and 1980s new halls were added; further displays are still being developed. At Middle Wallop the exhibition opened in a former cinema in 1974 but it was twelve years before funds for a new building were raised and this has since been extended.

Service museums in other European countries have experienced similar de-

Left: In 1940 a number of Gloster Gladiators of No 263 Squadron landed on the frozen waters of Lake Lesjaskog in Norway. The aircraft were left behind and sank when the ice melted. One was purchased by a local resident, who kept the biplane in a shed until 1977, when it was taken to Rygge Air Force Base for rebuilding. It is pictured here at Gardermoen, but it has now made the long journey to Bodø for display in the controversial new museum. (Bob Ogden)

Above: Only two examples of the General Aircraft Monospar survive. This excellently restored machine is on show at the Danmarks Flyemuseum at Billund; the other is under restoration at the Newark Air Museum in England. (Bob Ogden)

lays before they could be made ready. The excellent Swedish collection at Malmslatt owes its origins to Hugo Beckhammer, the commander of the base from 1941 to 1951. He had collected together a number of valuable aircraft and put them on show in a small hangar. After he retired he tried to get official support for his project but little was forthcoming. However, the local community of Ryd provided a building and around two dozen types were on show from 1967 to 1983. Finally in 1976 the plans for a museum were passed: the first stage was ready in 1984, the second following in 1989. Further expansion is hoped for so that a more comprehensive exhibition can be staged.

The Luftwaffe Museum, currently located at Ütersen but due to move to Gatow near Berlin, also owes its existence to the foresight of individuals. Private collections of items they had saved and aircraft provided by the Luftwaffe were put on show in two hangars which opened to the public in 1963. More aircraft were steadily acquired, and with unification several Soviet-built types used by the East German Air Force were moved to Ütersen.

The Danish Air Force maintains a collection of historic airframes but does not at present have the premises to display them, although the opening of the Danmarks Flyvemuseum at Billund in July 1990 had enabled some of them to be viewed by the public. This museum came about thanks to co-operation between a private preservation group and a commercial organization. In the Netherlands the Air Force did not open a museum until 1968, and this moved to a former army camp at Camp van Zeist in 1981 where two large halls were available.

One of the greatest controversies in recent years has taken place in Norway. The Air Force has been collecting historic aircraft at its bases since the 1960s. Volunteer teams restored many, and in 1984 several were moved to a former Luftwaffe hangar at Gardermoen, north of Oslo. The building had its problems and plans for a purpose-built museum were put forward. The choice of site was the subject of much debate and in November 1992 the Norwegian Parliament agreed to fund the building of a museum at Bodø in the far north of the country. The aircraft were put in store until the new premises were completed, and the facility was opened on 15 May 1994. Whilst many enthusiasts agree that Bodø should have a museum, they doubt the wisdom of placing the major Air Force museum in such a remote location.

In Italy similar problems have been encountered. In 1956 a small display was staged in the Rome area but in 1960 the International Exhibition in Turin resulted in some of the aircraft being moved to that city. When the fair closed one of the pavilions was taken over by the Air Force and some thirty aircraft were put on show, but public interest was disappointing and by the early 1970s the museum had all but closed. A restoration centre had meanwhile been set up at Vigna di Valle and political manoeuvrings resulted in this location being chosen for the site of the museum. At the former seaplane base on Lake Bracciano three historic hangars were still standing and modern extensions have now been constructed.

Military museums have also contributed to the preservation of important aircraft. The Musée Royal de l'Armée/Koninklijk Legermuseum in Brussels, housed in the vast Palace du Cinquantenaire complex, used to exhibit a huge amount of material, including some fifteen aircraft from the First World War period. The majority of these were suspended from the ceiling and remained untouched for half a century. A similar number of types from the 1940s and 1950s were stored in the adjoining former jousting hall. Eventually a plan to set up an aeronautical exhibition was approved and work started on the hall, including the removal of the sand floor. The aircraft in the military museum were taken down and restoration, largely by volunteers, began. Almost 100 aircraft are now contained in the vast hall and many more are in store. This exhibition of genuine First World War aircraft is one of the best, and exchanges with other collections have enhanced its appeal.

In Britain, the Imperial War Museum was established in 1920 and after a spell at South Kensington moved to Lambeth in 1935. During the early years items were lost, including some of the aircraft shown at the Islington exhibition. Second World War bombing caused further damage, and after the conflict only a small number of types were on show. By the 1960s space was at a premium and the donation of a North American Mustang from Canada resulted in the search for an additional site. The former RAF station at Duxford was acquired in 1971, and over the last two decades progress has been phenomenal. The surviving hangars from the 1930s at Duxford were refurbished, new ones have been erected and others have been moved to the site.

Duxford is a superb example of what can be achieved by sensible co-operation involving a national museum, private individuals and volunteers. The Duxford Aviation Society maintains a fleet of airliners at the airfield, and three collections of private airworthy machines are also on view. Stephen Grey's Fighter Collection, for example, makes up one of the most significant groups of airworthy Second World War (and just post-war) aircraft in the world. Deals have been struck with the Russian authorities, and a Lavochkin La-11 is now in a hangar and other Soviet types are promised. The Old Flying Machine Company, set up by Ray and Mark Hanna, has a number of Second World War aircraft and has recently acquired examples of some classic jet fighters, while Graham Warner's Aeroplane Restoration Company has rightfully achieved fame for its rebuilding of two Bristol Blenheims (although, sadly, the first of these crashed soon after its completion in 1987). Every visit to the airfield seems to reveal a new acquisition and in the restoration hangar progress is marked. Plans to construct a vast building to house the American aircraft will, it is hoped, come to fruition in the not too distant future.

Prior to the 1960s the museums of the Soviet Union and its satellite countries were something of a mystery to Western enthusiasts. Reports of exhibitions filtered out, and in the late 1940s there was an display of Second World War aircraft in Moscow. Sadly, as some of these were

Right: One of the many First World War types on show at the Musée Royal de l'Armée/Koninklijk Legermuseum in Brussels is this Royal Aircraft Factory R.E.8. A small number were supplied to Belgium after the end of the conflict. (Bob Ogden)

Right: The Lockheed U-2 first flew in 1955 but its existence was not revealed for several years. A number of U-2s have now been donated to museums, including this one, which arrived at the Imperial War Museum's Duxford site in 1992. (Bob Ogden)

of German, British and American origin they were later destroyed as the Cold War intensified and as fascist and capitalist products were deemed politically unsound. In 1960 the Soviet Air Force established a collection at its academy at Monino, east of Moscow; access was, to say the least, rather difficult, even for most Russians, and foreigners were admitted only after protracted negotiations. Over 100 aircraft are now on show at the Academy, the vast majority parked in the open air. The Central Military Museum in Moscow has a small number of aircraft on show and in recent years an exhibition of modern military machines has been set up at Khodynka airfield in the city, while the Civil Aviation Board has a collection of airliners at Ul'yanovsk. Details of other museums in the country emerged a few years ago and more are still being 'discovered'. Some of these are sited on military bases and access is restricted. The Northern Fleet maintains a superb collection of mainly Second World War types near Murmansk and the Pacific Fleet also has a collection.

During the late 1960s I was fortunate enough to gain access to museums in Czechoslovakia, Hungary and Poland and a few years later in East Germany. I have already mentioned the Technical Museum in Prague and the Kozlekedesi Muzeum in Budapest. Kbely, north-east of Prague, was the first military airfield in Czechoslovakia and in 1988 an air display to commemorate the 50th anniversary of Czech aviation was staged. A few years earlier the Military Museum had established a task force detailed to recover and preserve the historic aircraft which were scattered around the country. For the show, a number of these were put on view, and this led to the development of the air and space section of the museum. Initially one hangar was utilized, but with over eighty aircraft in the collection by 1972 only a few could be exhibited; today, the number is more than double that and three buildings together

Above: *The majority of the aircraft at the Air Force Museum at Monino near Moscow have to live outside in the harsh climate. This giant Antonov An-22 transport is one of the 100-plus types on view. (Bob Ogden)*

Right: *Among the former Deutsche Luftfahrt Sammlung aircraft which survived the Allies' raids on Berlin is the Messerschmitt Me 209 V1 in which Fritz Wendel set a world air speed record of 469.22mph on 26 April 1939. This historic aircraft awaits its turn in the restoration queue at the Muzeum Lotnictwa i Astronatyki at Krakow in Poland. (Bob Ogden)*

Above: The Air and Space Museum at Kbely has made rapid strides since its opening in 1968. A number of replicas and partial replicas have been constructed to fill gaps in the collection. Parts of the Avia Ba-122 aerobatic biplane flown in the 1930s by Frantisek Novak were found and the aircraft was rebuilt using original factory drawings. (Bob Ogden)

with an outside park are in use. The museum has constructed a number of replicas and also used original components in other rebuilding projects. The splitting of the country will inevitably result in some of the aircraft being moved to Slovakia.

The surplus of military aircraft arising from the collapse of communism has meant that several small private museums have appeared in former Czechoslovakia, Poland and, to a lesser extent, Hungary; military bases in these coun-

tries are also setting up museums. For several years the Military Museum in Budapest had aircraft on show in its courtyard but these were moved a decade ago. There are plans for an Air Force Museum just outside the city, and it is hoped that the Military Academy at Szolnok will open its collection to more visitors

One of the discoveries of the 1960s was the existence of the Muzeum Lotnictwa i Astronautyki at Krakow. In 1968 I was the second Westerner to visit the collection, which had been located by an Australian, Norman Wiltshire, while following up stories of a PZL P.11c which had been on show. The museum had led a nomadic existence in the post-Second World War years, but it officially came into being at Krakow in 1963. The P.11c was recognized as being from the famous Luftfahrtsammlung in Berlin, which had had more than 100 aircraft on view. The museum was bombed during the war and no aircraft were thought to have survived, but this was not the case – about twenty badly damaged airframes had been taken to eastern Germany and stored in railway carriages. Polish forces found the remains and realized their value, and eventually the relics arrived at Krakow. A restoration project in co-operation with the Museum für Verkehr und Technik in Berlin resulted in two being rebuilt, and others are now in workshops. The museum also displays a comprehensive range of indigenous aircraft and gliders.

In the last few years an exhibition of over fifty aircraft has been opened at Plovdiv in Bulgaria. On show is one of the three known surviving Arado Ar 196 floatplanes. This particular example was

for many years resident at the Naval Museum in Varna and its destruction was ordered by an ardent communist general; fortunately, it was spirited away and rebuilt for the new collection. There is a small military and technical museum in Sofia and also one in Bucharest in Romania. After many years of planning, the Yugoslav Aviation Museum opened at Belgrade Airport just before the outbreak of the ethnic conflicts. An excellent range of aircraft was on show and it is to be hoped that the establishment is still functioning.

Closed museums have not been solely the prerogative of the communist world: for many years the Spanish authorities placed historic machines in a hangar at Cuatro Vientos near Madrid. On the death of General Franco, however, the collection was opened on a regular basis and new buildings have been constructed and many more aircraft acquired.

One controversy which has raged in the preservation movement for years is whether historic aircraft should be flown or kept permanently grounded. There will always be crashes which may destroy a valuable machine, but the delight of seeing a vintage aircraft in its natural element is rewarding to pilot, mechanic and spectator. One of the first collections to be set up was that owned by Richard Shuttleworth. He acquired his first aircraft, a De Havilland Moth, in 1932 and built hangars and an airfield on the family estate at Old Warden in Bedfordshire. Up to the outbreak of the Second World War he collected several more aircraft and some were restored. He was killed in the conflict, but his mother established a trust to administer the collection and during the twenty years after the war further aeroplanes were acquired. The hangars were not opened to the public, but enthusiasts were given a warm wel-

come. In 1965 open days were held, when a selection of airworthy machines were flown, and the income from these and from film and television work raised funds to enable further hangars to be constructed. Now, a wander through these encompasses the early development of flight, from a 1910 Blériot, through First World War fighters and inter-war sporting aircraft, up to a Spitfire.

Jean Baptiste Salis in France bought a number of aircraft, including several using his war service gratuity, in 1918. In 1937 he purchased a plateau at Ardenay above the town of La Ferte Alais and constructed hangars and an airfield. During the war he hid many of his aircraft, but some were nevertheless lost during the German occupation. He died in 1967, but the tradition has been continued by his son Jean and now over 100 aircraft grace the field. The Salis Collection has stimulated the formation of several other preservation groups in France and many of these have been assisted by the Musée

Far left: The Nazi government used the Spanish Civil War for testing several military aircraft in combat conditions. A survivor is this Heinkel He 111E-1, which was restored to its original condition in the 1980s. It is pictured outside the original hangar at the Museo del Aire at Cuatro Vientos near Madrid. (Bob Ogden)

Above left: The Northern Aeroplane Workshops in Yorkshire built this Sopwith Triplane to the original specifications. Begun in the late 1970s, it was delivered to the Shuttleworth Collection at Old Warden in 1991. (Bob Ogden)

Left: Jean Salis has built a number of replicas and conversions for film work. In the late 1970s he modified two De Havilland Tiger Moths to represent Albatros Scouts from the First World War. The alterations were superficial, involving changes to the shape of the fuselage and tail surfaces. (Bob Ogden)

de l'Air, which has loaned aircraft and gliders and allowed them to be restored and flown. Collections of active aircraft are spreading throughout Europe: these principally involve light aircraft, but Second World War machines and also jet fighters and trainers are being added.

The 1960s in Britain saw the growth of the amateur preservation movement. After the destruction of many pre-war machines which were at the time considered worthless, efforts were made to save others. The Northern Aircraft Preservation Society (now the Aeroplane Collection) was formed in 1961 and by the end of the decade had been joined by more or-

ganizations; in 1967 the British Aircraft Preservation Council came into being. Over the last quarter of a century the fortunes of the groups have been mixed: some have fallen by the wayside; others have developed into excellent museums, open to the public on a regular basis. The Aeroplane Collection is still searching for a permanent home for its aircraft, but may now have found one at the former Hooton Park airfield on the Wirral. The Midland Air Museum at Coventry, the Newark Air Museum and the North East Air Museum at Sunderland all have large exhibition halls with substantial numbers of aircraft on view. Newer groups

Left: The Midland Air Museum officially opened its exhibition hall in 1991 but its superbly restored Gloster Meteor F.4 joined the collection somewhat earlier, in 1977. The building and the aircraft typify the progress made by some voluntarily run establishments. (Bob Ogden)

Right: Gliding has been to the forefront of aviation in Germany since the days of Otto Lilienthal. The historic hill site at the Wasserkuppe was first used in 1910. The Deutsches Segelflug Museum opened in 1970 and its new building was ready in 1987. Among the many classic designs on view is this Hans Jacobs-designed Rhonbussard. (Bob Ogden)

are always forming and no doubt some of these will flourish.

The older, established organizations are realizing that merely collecting airframes is only part of their function. Once the aircraft have been acquired, they have to be restored and maintained – an expensive and time-consuming business. Efforts over the last few years have been directed towards providing buildings and running the establishments as commercial concerns, although some of the newer groups appear to be having problems with planning. The preservation movement is active in many countries, the collections in France and Italy

being well organized by a central body. In Eastern Europe many new museums are springing up and the scene here is reminiscent of that in Britain in the 1960s.

Aviation museums can also be devoted to particular themes. There are two excellent collections devoted to rotary-wing flight – the Hubschrauber Museum at Bückeburg in Germany and the International Helicopter Museum at Weston-super-Mare in England. Glider museums include the Deutsches Segelflug Museum located on the historic Wasserkuppe Hill in Germany, the Segelflyg Museum in Sweden and the many collections in France. Exhibitions devoted to the prod-

ucts of one manufacturer are rare, but the Mosquito Museum at Salisbury Hall in England honours the work of the De Havilland company, while in Italy the Caproni family have managed to acquire suitable premises at Trento to exhibit the collection of aircraft designed by their father and other machines gathered together over the years. Several automobile museums include aircraft, perhaps just one mounted outside as an attraction even though it might not fit the theme of the display concerned. A number of what can only be called collections of junk have also acquired airframes.

The building of replica aircraft often arouses emotions. The term covers everything, from accurate reproductions using as nearly as possible the materials and building methods adopted by the original constructor, to mere shells that just follow the outlines. A number of museums have built static replicas to fill gaps in their collections and these vary in quality. The aircraft built for static work in films have joined many collections, and plastic Spitfires and Hurricanes are a new attraction in museums and on the gates of military establishments. Views are varied, but the removal of a genuinely historic aircraft from the latter duty is surely promoting the idea of preservation. Many vintage aircraft flying today have been almost totally rebuilt and often contain few original parts. These machines give their owners great pleasure, and when they visit air shows and rallies they are admired by many.

Very few countries seem to have adopted a national preservation policy. Finland, however, is one, and the results

of saving historic aircraft can be seen in museums throughout the country. Active aircraft have been earmarked to join the collections when their flying days are over. In Poland also, one of each type withdrawn from military service will be presented to the museum at Krakow.

With more than 700 museums and collections in Europe, there is much to be seen, and no doubt more such establishments will emerge when certain areas of the continent become politically more stable. It is difficult in a brief survey to present all aspects of the preservation movement, but I hope I have highlighted some of the significant ones.

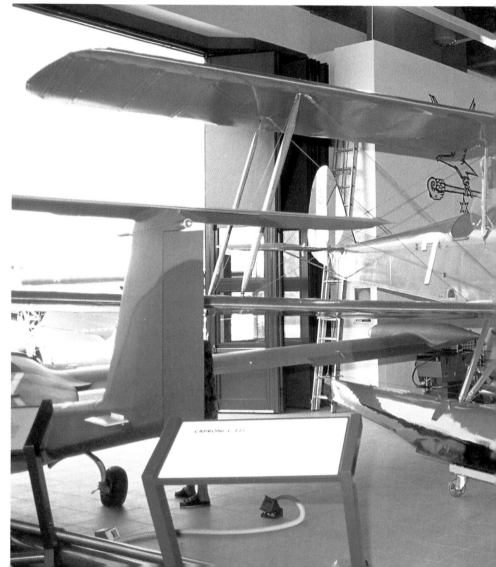

Aircraft Preservation in North America

Military aeroplanes have always been of tremendous interest to many North American people. Perhaps because of the vital role aircraft have played in US and Canadian military history, or because countless numbers of men and women have been involved with them, there will always be strong feelings for aircraft of this type.

Following the Second World War, before the smelting down of the vast numbers of aircraft remaining from the 300,000 built during the conflict, the US Government formed the War Assets Administration to sell the planes off to interested civilians and foreign governments. Fewer were sold than anticipated, even though they could be purchased fairly easily and at prices that today would be unheard of. For example, in 1951 war-surplus Lockheed P-38 Lightnings sold for just $1,250 and P-51 Mustangs for a mere $1,000, and if desired whole fleets of trainers, fighters and bombers could be acquired. To

Left, upper: The first aircraft to be built by the Air Force Factory in Finland was the A.22 floatplane, essentially a licence-built Hansa-Brandenburg W.33, of which over 120 were produced, serving from 1922 to 1936. The sole survivor is on view at the Suomen Ilmailumuseo, which is on the approach road to Helsinki Airport. (Bob Ogden)
Left: Gianni Caproni flew his first aircraft in 1910 and over the next seventy years companies bearing his name produced a wide variety of types. He founded a museum in 1929 and initially this consisted of his own designs; other aircraft were added in the 1930s, but during and after the Second World War some were lost. In October 1992 the first phase of a new museum at Trento was opened. Among the exhibits is this Caproni Ca 100 biplane dating from the 1930s. (Bob Ogden)

make it even more tempting, easy financial terms could be arranged; in fact, a noted Hollywood stunt pilot bought 475 such aircraft for the unbelievable sum of $55,000. What makes the whole matter interesting is that there was never any thought at the time that the aircraft sold under the plan would become as valuable as they are nor go on to become today's biggest source of airframes for the warbird market.

Long before these aeroplanes became the preserved aeronautical machinery of today, aircraft, and parts thereof, served many needs both on the ground and in the air. Enterprising persons fabricated storage buildings and goods wagons from fuselage shells and plenty of agricultural pumps were driven by Merlin and Allison engines. As flyers, these individuals took on both commercial and private roles, but, even though the planes were easy to obtain, numerous owners found them expensive to operate.

Although the disposal of Second World War aircraft has been well documented, this period of time did not mark the real beginning of man's passion for preserving historic flying machines. When the First World War came to an end, many foreign aircraft were brought back to North American soil as war souvenirs. Most were put into museums and private collections and some were kept airworthy. Still others were stored away in barns and hangars and, for the moment, forgotten. It was only in the early 1950s, however, that serious preservation caught hold, when people began to realize just how few of these historic aircraft remained.

Today, in spite of the high costs involved, the demand for these vintage aircraft has made their acquisition and restoration into both a hobby and a profession for many. In most cases the foremost purpose in obtaining them is the preservation of military aviation history, enhanced with the joy of flying a high-performance machine, but this is an opportunity limited to a select few.

The ways in which this preservation process is being accomplished are quite varied. Undoubtedly the most common means are the museums, which possess the largest number of both older and current aircraft, restored principally as nonflying exhibits. There are also individuals and associations whose primary aim is to acquire aircraft and rebuild them to flying condition. Still other people fabri-

Above: Aircraft are preserved in different ways. Some are used as gate guardians or as monuments to specific units or squadrons. Some even adorn the car parks of bars. (William Jesse)
***Right:** The unmistakable long-necked, canard-wing fuselage of the Valkyrie on display at the United States Air Force Museum. (William Jesse)*

cate airworthy replicas of aeroplanes that no longer exist.

The first American museum devoted solely to aviation was founded in 1923 at McCook Field near Dayton, Ohio, as a collection of US and foreign First World War aircraft and related equipment. In 1927, when McCook Field closed, the artefacts were moved to Wright Field and displayed in a corner of a laboratory building. Five years later the collection was renamed the Army Aeronautical Museum. In 1935 a new building to house the exhibits was erected, only to close during the Second World War. In 1948 the assortment of aeronautica, now known as the Air Force Technical Museum, was placed in a former engine overhaul facility, but it was not until 1954 that the doors were opened to the public, even though there were no complete aircraft on display. Soon after this entire airframes began to arrive and in 1956 the name was changed once more and the collection became the United States Air Force Museum.

During this period, in common with many aeroplane collections throughout the world, these rare souvenirs of history were being kept in outdated, even condemned buildings that were never intended to house such valuable items. At last, however, though the efforts of the Air Force Museum Foundation and the generosity of many contributors, the museum moved into its new home in 1971. It has since become one of the largest aircraft museums in the world and features the history of the US Air Force and its predecessor organizations, all the exhibits being chronologically presented.

Fly Past, Fly Present

One of the largest aircraft in the collection, the Convair B-36J, was the first aircraft to be placed in the new building, and with a wing span of 230 feet it was a snug fit, dwarfing all the other exhibits, including the big bombers from the Second World War. The oldest 'real' aeroplane in the Air Force Museum is the 1911 Wright 'Modified B' Flyer, an improved version of the Wright B Flyer, the first aeroplane to be produced and sold in quantity by the Wright Brothers. There is also a 1909 Wright Military Flyer, the first military heavier-than-air machine, but this is a reproduction which was built in 1955 by museum personnel. Probably the most exotic aircraft on display is the XB-70 Valkyrie bomber. Two of these six-engine giants were built by North American Aviation. Developed as a supersonic strategic bomber to succeed the B-52 and first flying in 1964, the XB-70 made little progress before it was cancelled. The museum's aircraft was delivered in 1969. Along with the unique there are the especially historic aircraft. *Bockscar*, the Boeing B-29 which dropped the atomic bomb on Nagasaki, is displayed, as is the Douglas A-1E Skyraider flown by Major Bernard Fisher in a dramatic rescue, in the midst of enemy soldiers, of a fellow pilot shot down over South Vietnam.

Below: There are few remaining examples of the Westland Lysander, one of the first STOL aircraft designed to operate from short, unprepared fields near the battle lines. This one forms part of the National Aviation Museum in Canada and has been preserved as a British Lysander I in the markings of No 110 Squadron RCAF while based in England. (William Jesse)

Below: The Canadian designed Noorduyn Norseman was intended as a bush plane but its versatility made it a popular aircraft with both the Canadian and the US military. (William Jesse)

Canada, a nation that has relied heavily on aircraft, more for its development than for its defence, recognized that its aviation heritage had to be contained in some form in order to show future generations just how crucial a role aviation has played. In 1964 the public was invited for the first time into three former Royal Canadian Air Force, Second World War hangars at Rockcliffe, a suburb of Ottawa, Canada's national capital. The compilation of aviation artefacts housed there was to become the National Aeronautical Collection. The collection dates back to 1919, when unofficial gathering of aircraft started with war souvenirs brought back from Europe for inclusion in different museums. Many of these aircraft, once reassembled, were put on display in various parts of Canada while others were actually flown at exhibitions throughout the country. Unfortunately, the fatal crash of a German aeroplane prompted the government to put a stop to all such flying; in fact, it even ordered the destruction of all flying war souvenirs, fearing further incidents. Luckily, many aircraft escaped this unhappy fate, mainly because they were not airworthy in the first place, while others, contained in the smaller, private collections across Canada, also survived. Fortunately, before all the surplus air-

Left: Many helicopters are restored in museums but few are returned to airworthiness. The Kaman HH-43B Huskie was a different type of machine, having unique, double-intermeshing rotor blades. This arrangement eliminated the need for the conventional stabilizing rotor mounted at the rear of the tail boom as on most other helicopters. (William Jesse)
Below: Awaiting the magic touch of the restorer are a Grumman F9F-2 and a North American B-25. In most cases, to achieve the desired results, magic translates into time and money – especially the latter. (William Jesse)

craft could be consigned to scrap, new government policies – which obviously caused some difficulties before they were agreed – came into effect and the remaining machines were put into storage for future consideration. In time, most of the aircraft, including those in private collections, fell into the hands of the government or the RCAF, generally through donation.

It was only in 1929 that a permanent Canadian aviation museum was officially established. However, on the outbreak of the Second World War the museum was closed and once more its contents were placed in storage. After the war the RCAF decided to resurrect the museum and, following the aims of its USAF counter-

Below right: One of the high points of an authentic restoration is to confirm the military history of an aircraft. There is little doubt about the history of this Texan. After serving with US forces it was flown by the Spanish Air Force and is now about to be rebuilt at one of the many facilities at the Chino airport in California. (William Jesse)

part, tried without success to preserve one of each aircraft type flown by the Air Force. Accommodation for the exhibits was found, but owing to constraints of space many other aircraft had to be displayed in secondary locations, including government buildings and airport terminals. In spite of the effort, the entire collection still lacked a proper home. In the meantime more aircraft were being added to the collection, most ending up in storage.

When the RCAF moved out of Rockcliffe the vacant hangars became the best location to exhibit the remainder of the stored items and by 1959 all the aircraft at the site had been moved to their new home, heralding the beginnings of a bona fide aviation museum containing both civilian and military aircraft and a variety of aero-engines. However, although a new home had been found, the

museum suffered from the same problem as the USAF Museum – the buildings were not ideal. Like many older hangars, those at Rockcliffe were constructed of wood and consequently offered little protection from fire. Fear of such a fiery disaster led museum officials once more to seek improved housing for their valuable exhibits.

In 1982 the Canadian Government approved $20 million for the construction of new museum buildings. The first of three planned structures, each incorporating the latest in environmental protection measures for the aircraft and displays, was opened to the public in 1988 and today the collection's new home contains some fifty aircraft, from both world wars, commercial aviation and replica aircraft – including a reproduction of the AEA Silver Dart, the first aircraft in Canada to make a powered flight, which

took place in February 1909. One of the most popular attractions is a cockpit section of the supersonic Avro CF-105 Arrow, one of the most controversial aircraft projects in Canadian history. At the moment there are about 70 aircraft and literally tons of aero-engines and parts still in storage.

As might be expected, the majority of older aircraft that end up in museums are not in the best of shape, and some type of restoration is normally required before they can be displayed. Most museums have a restoration department to carry out the repair, preservation and reconstruction of the artefacts that fall under their jurisdiction. This work, while of great interest, is seldom seen by the public. The restoration of aircraft compo-

nents presents no greater difficulties than the restoration of other historic objects, but what has been discovered is that since aircraft frequently contain so many diverse materials – wood, metal and fabrics including cotton, silk and linen, all combined with various kinds of paint, enamels and adhesives – authentic refurbishment is a complex undertaking. Parts can be repaired or restored using the correct methods provided the necessary material is still available. There are times when parts need to be fabricated, but it is not practicable to possess every type of tool needed for these operations and the work is generally subcontracted out. Another means of obtaining particular components is through negotiation with other museums, buying parts or exchang-

Right: Is it 1941 or is it today? So devoted are some enthusiasts that they even try to include accessories of the period. (William Jesse)

Left: *The Harvard or T-6 Texan was one of the most famous training aircraft of the Second World War and today it is one of the most popular of all preserved military aircraft. (William Jesse)*

ing pieces not required for those that are. The donation of any aircraft part to a museum is always gratefully accepted, for it can always be used, now or some time in the future.

The first restoration at the National Aviation Museum involved a Curtiss JN-4 and was carried out from 1962 to 1964. Following a standard restoration practice, work proceeded on the basis that parts be preserved rather than restored, restored rather than replaced, and replaced only when absolutely necessary. Thus original parts were used wherever possible. In some cases a piece of new material could be spliced into an old part so as to keep the part as original as possible ≈ provided that the new material was of the same type. Wings and tail surfaces could be covered using linen as on the original instead of modern synthetic cov-

erings. The only time these standards would vary was in the use of up-to-date adhesives and paints, and in the use of modern plastics for window material. The JN-4, when received by the museum, was essentially complete, even to the 1918 fabric on the wings, but it had seen civilian use and much of the instrumentation had been altered. All in all, however, it represented a great effort as a first project.

Besides the government-funded museums, there are also a fair number of private museums and collections, especially in the United States. The Pima Air Museum in Tucson, Arizona, located on nearly 75 acres of desert land, has a vast collection of aeroplanes and helicopters and is in the fortunate position of being situated literally next door to the Davis-Monthan Air Force Base. For many years thousands of military aircraft have been

stored, dismantled or scrapped at Davis-Monthan, and some years back examples of the many aircraft that had passed through the base were lined up near its entrance. Over time they attracted many sightseers, even though the site was not officially open to the public. This interest led to a proposal for establishing a museum in the area that would benefit from the vast resources available on the spot.

In 1969 the Pima collection acquired 35 Air Force aircraft which the Military Aircraft Storage and Disposition Center, part of the Davis-Monthan operation, had displayed at the perimeter of the base and these became the nucleus of the museum which was opened to the public in 1976. The Pima facility is currently the largest

privately financed air museum in existence. There are more than 200 aircraft from all generations, including some rare examples not seen elsewhere, such as the North American F-107A (one of three built), the Columbia XJL-1 seaplane, an early Grumman design and the three-engine Northrop YC-125A Raider. Arizona is well known for its moderate climate and hard, corrosion-deterring, alkaline

Below: Maybe a 'basket case' to some, but worth its weight in gold: a Harvard Mk II centre-section awaits its rebuild. (William Jesse)
Right: Restored in the livery of the 330th Bomb Group of the Twentieth Air Force with which it flew, the Boeing B-29 Superfortress at the Pima Museum holds court when Second World War crews have their reunions there. (William Jesse)

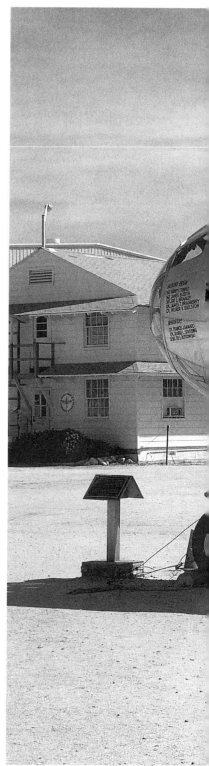

soil, all of which enable most aircraft to be displayed out of doors, although the most fragile airframes are kept inside one of the three hangars that have a combined display space of over 60,000 square feet.

Much of the rebuilding of the Pima collection takes place in public view at the museum's outdoor workshops, where anything from rebuilding a basket case to a simple paint restoration is accomplished. As in all rejuvenation projects, progress is slow, requiring painstaking attention, but the effort is well rewarded, with more and more exhibits being placed on display each month, looking as good as when they were in operational service.

To many, all historical aircraft, and especially the very rare ones, should be cloistered safely in a museum – even though they may have been restored to flying condition. On the other hand, there are those who feel that the only place to display this living history is in the skies. The latter groups are made up of people like the Texas-based Confederate Air Force, founded in the early 1950s when a number of pilots got hold of some surplus fighters, and the Valiant Air Command, formed in Florida in 1977 when twelve warplane owners got together to make a dream come true. These are the organizations whose enthusiasm for actual airborne history never dwindles, in spite of apparently insurmountable odds. Much the same can be said of the National Warplane Museum in New York State, an association dedicated to preserving and flying vintage military aircraft, including those from the Korean War. The air-

Right: Although it can be an exasperating experience, preservation to total authenticity is the goal. (William Jesse)

Left: Replicas are built when originals are virtually non-existent, as in the case of the North American NA-50. Designed as a fighter, this aircraft was produced only in very small numbers and today's versions are constructed around Texan or Harvard airframes. (William Jesse)

craft of the NWM are more than mere hulks on static display: the majority of the planes fly regularly and the reconstruction of others to flying status is a continuing activity.

At the outset of the Second World War, with Britain's close proximity to Europe and her airfields clogged with fighters and bombers, an alternative location for flying training had to be established. The British came to Canada and set up the British Commonwealth Air Training Plan, which would ultimately become responsible for the training of thousands of Allied airmen. Student pilots earned their wings on a variety of basic training aircraft, including the most famous of all – the Harvard. Today the Canadian Harvard Aircraft Association, based at Tillsonburg in Ontario, has cho-

sen to keep the spirit of the BCATP alive by acquiring, preserving and flying the Harvard and other aircraft associated with the Plan. In existence since 1985, the CHAA is a flying museum that operates, along with the Harvard, a Yale and a Tiger Moth. It has a worldwide membership of well over 300.

As the interest in surplus aircraft grew, so did the demand for them, and anything that flew with any military ties whatsoever was ripe for restoration. With so few aircraft available to begin with, however, it was inevitable that there would come a time when the supply would dry up. Associations thus began to be formed whose sole purpose was to research and find such planes, be they abandoned wrecks, submerged under water or still on the strength of Third World

military air forces – airframes and wreckage that could be, with a lot of imagination and even more money, painstakingly rebuilt to flying status. So great has been the demand for these aircraft that remains pulled from watery graves or removed from beneath tons of earth or ice have been deemed historic enough to warrant restoration. To some, a wreck with just a few usable parts becomes a gold mine. The armed forces of some small countries are still flying what we would consider vintage military aircraft, although their numbers are quite small. Over the years, many of these airframes have been returned to North America and quickly snapped up by enthusiasts. Of course, everyone dreams of finding a Second World War aircraft languishing in an old barn, although those days are, sadly, long gone. The renewed interest in preserving surplus aircraft has prompted the establishment of restoration facilities specializing in Second World War planes. Those in California, particularly around Chino, have a good reputation for this type of work, but many top-quality projects have emerged from other workshops throughout the continent, for example in Florida, Texas and British Columbia.

As with any preservation project, the first concern of the rebuilder is the finished product – will it be a sporty aerial hot rod with few concessions to authenticity or will it become an aircraft faithfully resurrected, in its correct military markings? Thankfully, the demand for the former is on the decline. To achieve the latter involves a good deal of preparation, including, if possible, a look into the subject's military background. Records

are examined, log books read, and there are even attempts to find original photographs and talk to personnel who may at one time have been associated with the machine. It is not an easy task, but the rewards are great when everything comes together.

But, despite the demand for one hundred per cent authenticity, it is obvious that, unlike the preservation of aircraft for static display, the restoration of an airworthy machine cannot always follow the 'purist' theories outlined earlier. There is, today, a sort of artistic licence – obligatory when one considers the labour required to upgrade original technology and, even more difficult, locate all the necessary original parts (which could take a lifetime, even if it were possible at all). Clearly, the more authentic the restoration the higher the dollar value of the end product, but with today's technology, materials and avionics it makes little sense to ignore their potential. Common sense and safety do apply, and the result is that these 'old' aeroplanes are more often than not better built than they were fifty years ago.

Finally, after what seems like an eternity and the preservation work is complete, what becomes of the aircraft? Without doubt, every pilot of a warbird wants to fly it as much as he can afford to, so it is unlikely to sit idly in a hangar, nor will it be flown spasmodically, alone in a sky laden with conventional, Wichita-built machines. Perhaps the best way of enjoying an aircraft of this nature is to fly it in the company of others, to participate in an event where other pilots of preserved warbirds have something in common. In

Above: *One military aircraft very rare today is the Japanese A6M Zero. Many replicas were, however, built for use in such films as Tora! Tora! Tora! and Midway. Today they play 'the enemy' in many air shows. (William Jesse)*

1962 the Confederate Air Force held the first of what was to become an annual event. To show off their newly acquired Republic P-47 Thunderbolt, the 'self-appointed colonels' of the CAF held an air show. That was the door-opener, and each year since then ex-military aircraft have flown in from all parts of the country to what has become a tremendous gathering of vintage aeroplanes. So popular did the CAF and its aircraft become that they received countless invitations to attend other shows across the country.

Today, air shows of this nature are very popular, and seldom does a month pass without two or three such events. Each association attempts to stage one, usually to aid the funding of restoration projects. Generally a theme is adopted, based perhaps on a historic event or the anniversary of a famous squadron; thus in 1991 the attack on Pearl Harbor was remembered and in 1994 the D-Day invasion was commemorated. Aircraft from all over the continent attend, and before the flying begins enthusiasts may inspect

them, ask questions and of course take photographs. By early afternoon the motors come to life and the propellers start turning. The highlights of most shows include the re-enactment of aerial battles, where a progression of trainers, fighters and transports fly in formation, simulate dogfights or carry out 'strafing runs'. The finale features all of the bombers in the air simulating drops on 'enemy targets', the dastardly tanks and battleships – typically constructed from plywood – being destroyed in a barrage of awesome pyrotechnics and billowing smoke.

One of the exciting (and obviously well-rehearsed) routines is the 'Tora! Tora! Tora!' demonstration, wherein a dozen or so 'Japanese' aircraft 'attack' the airfield, air raid sirens wailing in the background, and a 'squadron' of P-40s and Wildcats scrambles to intercept them. One by one, the 'shot down' 'enemy' aircraft, trailing smoke, disappear behind a hill or copse, only to recover on another runway out of sight of the spectators – tremendous action and a lot of very skilful flying. Once all is back to normal (if that is at all possible, given the excitement), the flying portion of the show is sometimes closed by a flypast in the 'missing man' formation. As the four fighters pass the centre of the show, one aircraft pulls up, leaving a gap in the formation, as a reminder of all those military personnel from all wars who made the supreme sacrifice – all in all, a spectacular end to what has normally been a three- or four-hour flying display.

Throughout the day there are scores of vendors selling everything relating to aviation, from cloth patches (the proceeds from which generally go towards preserving and maintaining the aeroplanes) to aircraft themselves, models or the real things, complete or in various stages of preservation. Without a doubt, air shows are the best way to get warbirds and enthusiasts together – be they full-blown events which include modern military and civilian planes or just a simple gathering of vintage machines at which the owners share each other's joys and headaches and savour the camaraderie.

It is obvious that the Second World War aircraft movement is alive and well, but what about those people whose interest in aviation concerns earlier machines, perhaps going back to the First World War or before? Or the owners of rare antiques of which only a handful of parts exist? To get such relics back into the air is not an easy task. They have become extremely scarce, and, besides, the fragile state of aeroplanes so old often necessitates the building of a reproduction. Although they are not yet as popular as their Second World War counterparts,

there is a growing fascination for these machines and dozens of replicas are being built at a frantic pace. The interest has spawned a proliferation of industries supplying builders' plans and remanufactured parts, often encouraging the amateur to construct his own aeroplane. Like most rebuilt warbirds of the Second World War, these reproductions usually take advantage of modern technology, most notably in respect of their power-plants. Rare original engines, especially rotaries, are hard to find and unreliable to say the least, and thus some of today's replicas are powered by automobile motors.

And what about the Second World War aircraft that no longer survive in any shape or form? There is a demand for these too, especially some of the European and Japanese types. Many replica Japanese fighters and bombers have been built over the years by the film industry to fly in *Tora! Tora! Tora!*, *Midway* and similar productions. These aircraft are generally built around existing vintage airframes, particularly the North American Texan and the Consolidated Vultee. While it is obvious that replica aeroplanes cannot have the authentic historical credentials that a genuine warbird possesses, this does not really bother the builders or the pilots For motion pictures the requirement is to build a 'close-enough' copy that can easily lure the non-expert into believing that it is the real thing. As for the First World War replicas, it seems

Left: A pair of Mustangs over Florida. Most people seem to prefer to see these rare warplanes in the air rather than displayed in a museum. (William Jesse)

Left: 'Curses! It's the evil Red Baron!' A Fokker Triplane from the Great War Flying Museum taxies out to do battle. (William Jesse)

that historical fidelity takes second place to the sheer fun of open-cockpit flying – and if the machine resembles something flown by the Red Baron, or Snoopy for that matter, then so much the better!

The Great War Flying Museum (developed from the Ontario Aviation Historical Society) is situated north of Toronto and the members devote their time and talents to recreating the sights, sounds and feel of First World War flying. Their fleet of British and German aeroplanes was built by the members in their own hangar. Weather permitting, the old biplanes and triplanes are flown regularly, visiting air shows within range. The museum also includes a collection of artefacts, memorabilia and uniforms from the First World War.

Will there come a time when all hope of rebuilding an old fighter or trainer will be non-existent? Even though many of the restored military planes of today con-

tain reproduction components, the idea of building a one hundred per cent new P-47 or Corsair is still a long way off, although it is being attempted. Perhaps one day a 'new' Second World War aircraft will appear. What will happen when there are no longer any vintage aircraft available for restoration? In a sense the future is now, and the aircraft of interest are those newer-generation, often turbine-powered surplus planes from the Korea and Vietnam eras. Still another potential source for ex-military planes, and one which is already being explored in great detail, is the former Iron Curtain countries. At present the more modern military equipment seems to be available, but rumours persist that there may be some vintage aircraft out there as well.

In conclusion, why do people collect, restore and preserve vintage aeroplanes? Is there a rational explanation as to why adult men and women spend thousands

Below: As the amount of warbird stock diminishes, more and more surplus military aircraft are coming to North America from countries formerly behind the Iron Curtain. Some of the aircraft are old but more are relatively recent. (William Jesse)

of dollars and a good part of their lives urging these venerable machines back into the skies? Possibly the real reason can only be found in the satisfaction with which the hobby provides them – to know that the old airframe and stack of parts that seem to have been there for ever and have taken all of their spare time to assemble have finally been converted into an airworthy, historic flying machine, a flying machine that has perhaps played a vital role in a nation's history and has perhaps never been seen by most people. By the same token, there are those who feel that there has been enough conflict in the world and that to preserve these machines is to glorify war. Perhaps things

are best summed up by the colonels of the Confederate Air Force:

'We believe that the war years should be remembered not only for their impact on history but for the lessons they contain for present and future generations. And this requires a looking back – artefacts, stories re-told and dramatized. These flying machines are precious relics of a time that changed the world for ever. We are not just salvaging a few noble old warplanes, but preserving intact some of the million memories of history's most awesome and horrible armed conflict. By keeping these memories alive we may be able to prevent it from ever happening again.'

Antiques at Old Warden

They say that time flies at Old Warden, and enthusiasts of first-generation 'stick and string' aircraft would certainly agree that the Shuttleworth Collection is without doubt the finest of all assemblages devoted to early aircraft.

The Collection's history dates back to the 1800s when Joseph Shuttleworth, the owner of a boat-building business on the River Witham, went into partnership with Nathaniel Clayton, an iron foundry owner based in Lincoln. They embarked upon the production of semi-portable, steam-powered farm threshing machinery which could be transported into fields, thus avoiding the need to move crops into the farmyard. Having placed their entire capital in the project, they were delighted when the product succeeded, and the Stamp End works in Lincoln expanded to cover twenty acres, employing a workforce of 2,000. Some 25,000 machines, including self-propelled traction engines, were produced there and in London – and also in Vienna, where the Shuttleworthstrasse was named in honour of the nearby works.

Clayton and Shuttleworth also had business agencies in the Baltic states, in South America, in Australia and on the African continent, and Joseph Shuttleworth became a respected and wealthy benefactor both in Lincoln and in Bedfordshire, where he purchased the 7,000-acre Old Warden Park some 45 miles north of London. Joseph died in 1883, leaving his estates in Lincolnshire to his elder son and those in Bedfordshire to the younger Frank, who was at the time a 38-year-old major in the 7th Hussars.

In 1902 Frank married Dorothy Clotilda Lang, and just nine days before Louis Blériot crossed the English Channel, on 16 July 1909, she gave birth to Richard Ormonde Shuttleworth. Following Frank's death in 1913, Richard was brought up by Dorothy and her family retainers. At the age of thirteen the boy joined Eton College – and more particularly its School of Mechanics – and his early liking for machinery quickly developed: the young Shuttleworth had a reputation for arriving late for lessons and for his appearances at cricket matches covered in oil and grease. However, he opted to follow his father's path into the Army and entered Sandhurst, passing out 14th in his entry of 26 as a second lieutenant in the 16th/5th Lancers.

The first of many purchases in what would become the Shuttleworth Collection was of an 1897 Panhard et Levassor which had competed in the Paris–Amsterdam Race in 1898 and which he entered in the 1928 London to Brighton run. In 1932 he inherited the fortune of a childless uncle together with a further benefit from his father's will, and this £2 million sum – equivalent to some £50 million today – made Richard one of the wealthiest men in England.

Although Old Warden is now famous for its vintage aircraft, Richard's early purchases were all ground based: a 1903 De Dietrich 24hp Racer, a 5hp Baby Peugeot and an 1898 Benz International, as well as a 1903 Locomobile, a Shand Mason steam fire engine, a Clayton & Shuttleworth Colonial traction engine and an Aveling Barford 7-ton O Type Tandem Roller; this last was usefully em-

Above: Shuttleworth doing what it knows best: the 1916 Sopwith Pup airborne at one of the Collection's regular and justly famous flying days. (Shuttleworth Collection/Air Portraits) Right: Another example of why Old Warden is a mecca for fans of preserved aviation. The Gloster Gladiator carries No 247 Squadron markings and is the only flying example of the type in the world. (Shuttleworth Collection/Air Portraits)

ployed to flatten out the base of his new aerodrome at Old Warden, where Richard intended to pursue his developing interest in flying machines. His first acquisition here was a 1920 DH 60 Hermes Moth which he bought for £300 and learned to fly through a mixture of professional lessons and self-tuition. Further purchases reflect the formative years of aviation: a Comper Swift, an Avro Avian, a Blackburn Velos torpedo bomber and a Vickers Vimy, together with a DH Dragon from The King's Flight and a small number of Desoutter Monoplanes which he often used for Channel-hopping flights to pick up Bugatti spares. (Richard was also interested in motor racing. He regularly raced at Brooklands, and in October 1935 he won the Donington Grand Prix. In the South African Grand Prix his Alfa Romeo

Inventory of Aeroplanes at Old Warden Aerodrome

Type	Date	Remarks
Blériot XI*	1901	G-AANG, BAPC 3, C/N 14; believed to be the earliest genuine aeroplane with the earliest aero-engine flying
Deperdussin*	1910	G-AANH, BAPC 4; sole surviving example
Bristol Boxkite	1910	Replica built for film *Those Magnificent Men in their Flying Machines*
Avro Triplane IV	1911	Replica built for film *Those Magnificent Men in their Flying Machines*
Blackburn Monoplane Type D*	1912	Sole surviving example and earliest genuine airworthy British aircraft
Sopwith Pup	1916	Built as Sopwith Dove and converted by Richard Shuttleworth
Sopwith Triplane	1916	Constructed by Northern Aeroplane Workshops 1970–90; carries No 8 Naval Sqn markings
Avro 504K	1918	Sole surviving airworthy example in Europe
Bristol Fighter	1918	Sole surviving airworthy example, with earliest Rolls-Royce aero-engine flying
RAF S.E.5a	1918	
LVG C.VI	1918	Sole surviving flyable example of a German WWI two-seat aircraft
Sopwith Dove	1919	Constructed by Skyport Engineering; on loan
EE Wren	1923	Sole surviving example
De Havilland 23 Humming Bird	1923	Prototype DH 23; earliest DH type flying and earliest prototype of any kind flying
De Havilland 51	1924	Sole surviving example
De Havilland 60 Cirrus Moth	1925	Earliest DH 60 worldwide; on loan
De Havilland 60X Moth*	1928	Richard Shuttleworth's first aeroplane
Hawker Tomtit	1928	Sole surviving example
Parnall Elf	1929	Sole surviving example
Southern Martlet	1929	Sole surviving example; under restoration
Blake Bluetit	1929	Sole example; under restoration
De Havilland 60G Moth	1930	
De Havilland 80A Puss Moth	1930	On loan
Desoutter Monoplane*	1930	Under restoration; National Flying Service markings
Granger Archaeopteryx	1930	Sole surviving example; capable only of taxying
Avro 621 Tutor	1931	Sole surviving flyable example
De Havilland 82A Tiger Moth	1931	
Arrow Active	1932	Sole surviving example; on loan
Cierva C 30A	1934	Capable only of taxying
Mignet HM 14 'Flying Flea'	1934	Capable only of taxying
De Havilland 88 Comet	1934	*Grosvenor House*; sole surviving example; restored to flying condition 1973–87; flying suspended April 1994 but maintained in airworthy condition
Gloster Gladiator	1934	Sole surviving airworthy example; carries No 247 Sqn markings
Hawker Hind	1934	Sole surviving airworthy example; ex-Royal Afghan Air Force; carries No XV Sqn markings
Percival Gull Six	1935	Aircraft of Jean Batten and first solo flight from England to New Zealand; rebuilt 1986–90
BA Swallow	1935	
De Havilland 87B Hornet Moth	1936	Carries No 3 Coastal Patrol Flight markings of WWII service
Miles M14A Magister	1937	
Supermarine Spitfire VC	1941	Carries No 310 (Czech) Sqn markings; full career documents
DHC-1 Chipmunk	1946	Carries Oxford University Air Sqn markings

Notes

Aircraft marked thus * are those collected by Richard Shuttleworth himself. The years quoted are those of the type's first flight. In addition to the aircraft listed above, the following aircraft are currently (1994) undergoing rebuilding or restoration: Hawker Sea Hurricane IB (at Duxford), the sole surviving example of a Sea Hurricane and fitted with the earliest example of Merlin engine extant; a Bristol Monoplane M1C (at Mirfield, Yorkshire), a reproduction of a radical design of 1916, of which only 125 were built; and a Sopwith Camel of 1916 (also at Mirfield). In addition, a 1939 Gloster Sea Gladiator is on loan to the Fleet Air Arm Museum at Yeovilton and an ANEC II of 1924 – the sole surviving example, built for trials – is in storage.

Above: This superb biplane from the Shuttleworth Collection is a 1918 S.E.5a, one of the most successful scouts of the 1914–18 War and truly a classic aircraft that fully deserves this magnificent restoration. (Shuttleworth Collection/Air Portraits)

went out of control and he was forced to bail out, landing on a boulder and sustaining head injuries together with a severely damaged leg. Doctors feared that he would not survive the accident, but after nineteen days he regained consciousness and after a long period of convalescence he resumed racing.)

The Collection continued to grow. Richard soon purchased his first monoplane, a 1909 Blériot XI, followed by a 1910 Deperdussin, both of which he flew at RAF displays at Hendon, at Royal Aeronautical Society garden parties and at Cranfield Empire Air Days. During a holiday in Belgium he purchased a First World War Hanriot fighter which he flew back to Old Warden, only to crash-land the machine later following a spirited display over the airfield, having mistaken as encouragement the ground crew's attempts to indicate that he had lost a wheel! He obtained a 1915 Avro 504K to sell joy rides to the public, and a Sopwith Dove which, remarkably, he converted back to its 1916 single-seat Pup configuration. The superb 1912 Blackburn Monoplane that is now a star attraction at Shuttleworth was actually found buried under a hayrick. Today it is the earliest genuine airworthy British aircraft in existence.

Richard also set up The Aeronautical Advertising Company, together with the Warden Aviation and Engineering Company, briefly experimenting with neon signs attached to his DH Dragon. He received interest from companies such as Whitbread, but complaints from the public over the 'desecration of the night sky and the disturbance of the peace of the evening' encouraged the Government to enforce unreasonably high minimum flying altitudes (often above cloud). Bedfordshire County Council was also less than sympathetic to Richard's enthusiasm, rejecting his offer – Richard was also a Councillor – to allow 60 acres of his estate near Bedford to be used, free of charge, as a municipal airport.

At the age of 29, and despite a hearing impediment caused by his motoring accident in South Africa, Richard joined the Royal Air Force Volunteer Reserve following the Munich Crisis in 1938. He eventually joined the Central Flying School at Upavon, where he flew Bristol Blenheims before being posted to No 12 Operational Training Unit at Benson. Here he built upon his 1,000 hours of private flying, this time on the Fairey Battle. During the night of 1–2 August 1940 he was assigned to Battle L4971 for a night cross-country training flight but soon after he took off he was recalled in response to deteriorating weather. Frustrated because of the near-perfect conditions back at base, he took off again for some local flying. Shortly after departing from Benson, he dis-

Above: A truly magnificent sight: the sole surviving airworthy Hawker Hind flies from Old Warden, bearing the markings of No XV Squadron. The aircraft is actually an ex-Royal Afghan Air Force example (Shuttleworth Collection/Air Portraits)

Left: The famous 1934 De Havilland 88 Comet Grosvenor House *of air race fame. Members of the public can get very close to the actual restoration and maintenance of aircraft at Old Warden. (Shuttleworth Collection/Air Portraits)*

appeared into the developing clouds and a few minutes later his Battle crashed. Pilot Officer Shuttleworth was later found, having been thrown clear of the crashed aircraft but dead from multiple injuries. Richard's funeral took place at St Leonard's Church, overlooking Old Warden.

Dorothy was devastated by the loss of her son, and she dedicated her time to a Red Cross Convalescent Home and Auxiliary Hospital set up in the family house during the war. Richard had bequeathed everything to her in his will, and Mrs Dorothy Shuttleworth OBE decided to use his legacy to provide a centre for agricultural training and for the promotion of education and training in the science, practice and history of aviation and

automotive transport. She established the Richard Ormonde Shuttleworth Remembrance Trust in 1944, and non-aviation activities are now conducted by the Shuttleworth Agricultural College, based in the vast country house that was once the family home. The full collection of vehicles and aircraft was first opened to the public in 1964, and since then the airfield has been improved to incorporate more hangars, a restaurant/cafeteria and a gift shop.

Although some of the aircraft and vehicles from Richard's original collection have been disposed of, many remain at Old Warden, having been joined by many other classic designs, including the replica Bristol Boxkite and Avro Triplane featured in the film *Those Magnificent*

Men in their Flying Machines and a Bristol Fighter powered by the earliest Rolls-Royce aero-engine still operational anywhere in the world. The 1924 DH 51 is the oldest De Havilland design still flying, and other significant aircraft include a beautiful Hawker Hind retrieved from Afghanistan and a Supermarine Spitfire VC.

From May to October monthly flying displays are held at Old Warden, although the Collection is open to the public all week. Naturally, the air shows and Twilight Aerial Displays are particularly popular with the public, affording a rare opportunity for them to see many of the Shuttleworth aircraft take to the air: as is not the case with many aviation museums, virtually every exhibit at Old Warden is airworthy. Many of the aircraft are unique, for example the 1909 Blériot XI,

which is probably the oldest flyable aircraft, and has the oldest operational aero-engine, in the world today. The small but professional team of engineering staff ensure that the aeroplanes are maintained in top class condition for appearances not only over Old Warden but also further afield at venues such as Duxford, Mildenhall and Finningley. The monthly air displays include outside participants such as warbirds from Duxford and rather more modern aircraft from the RAF: it is not impossible to see a Sopwith Pup immediately followed by a Panavia Tornado, and over the years the skies over Old Warden have been visited by many classic aircraft such as the Vulcan, Varsity, Shackleton, Gannet, Lancaster and, of course, the *Red Arrows*.

Almost 100,000 people visit Old Warden every year, and the Shuttleworth

Below: Proving that not just aircraft are present at Old Warden, this photograph shows an original Hucks Starter alongside the Hind. Both display the attention to detail and care that is the Shuttleworth Collection's hallmark. (Shuttleworth Collection/ Air Portraits)

Collection remains one of the world's foremost aviation museums, home to a variety of historic aircraft and the venue for a regular series of fascinating aerial displays. Increasing costs have forced a reassessment of exactly how the Collection is to be maintained in the future. Over 90 per cent of its income is generated from the air displays, and although poor weather can halt flying the costs have continually to be met and so the business is finely balanced. Certain aircraft have had to be sold over the years – the Spitfire PR.XI and the Auster AOP.9 are examples – but choosing which aircraft to dispose of is not a pleasant task. Factors in making such a decision include whether the type is a gift, is of historical significance, is popular with the public and of

course whether it is an original Richard Shuttleworth possession. However, it is a sad but unavoidable fact that even world famous museums such as this one have to be run as successful business concerns if they are to continue to delight enthusiasts. Membership of the Shuttleworth Veteran Aeroplane Society is increasingly demonstrating how these enthusiasts can have a real impact on the world of preserved aviation.

Nevertheless, time really does fly at Old Warden, figuratively on the ground, where the aircraft and museum exhibits are available for close inspection, and in the air, where Richard Shuttleworth believed that classic aeroplanes should be seen whenever possible . . . and at Old Warden it *is* possible!

Stories of Restoration

Nicholas Veronico/Tim Laming

During the Second World War Grumman Aircraft Engineering, of Bethpage, New York, built 12,275 single-seat F6F Hellcats in day fighter, night fighter, and photo-reconnaissance variants. Introduced into combat in the Pacific Theatre during September 1943, the Hellcat cut its teeth flying from the USS *Yorktown* during attacks on the Marcus Islands. It was flown by the US Navy and Marine Corps and the Royal Navy's Fleet Air Arm.

Two major Hellcat models were built. The F6F-3 was powered by a 2,000-horsepower Pratt & Whitney R-2800-10 supercharged, 18-cylinder, radial engine driving a Hamilton Standard 13 foot 1 inch diameter, three-blade propeller. Armed with six .50-calibre machine guns and carrying heavy armour plating to protect the pilot and aircraft systems, the Hellcat could take a substantial number of hits and deliver a tremendous amount of firepower. The most numerous version of the Hellcat was the F6F-5, which featured a water-injected R-2800-10W engine in a redesigned cowling, a strengthened airframe and a flat, bullet-proof windscreen

and could carry up to 2,000lb of bombs and six 5-inch rockets. Night fighter versions, designated F6F-3N and -5N, were also constructed.

During the war years the Hellcat chalked up an impressive kill tally: carrier-based Hellcats downed 4,947 Japanese aircraft while land-based F6Fs shot down and additional 209. Almost 75 per cent of the US Navy and Marine Corps fighter aces flew the Hellcat. Production ended in November 1945 when the last example was delivered to the Navy. Hellcats were phased out of Naval Reserve squadrons and permanently retired from service in 1956.

Today only 22 Hellcats survive, and only seven of those are capable of flying. In 1986 the Lone Star Flight Museum acquired an F6F-5 that had been on display in another museum and began the most comprehensive restoration of a Hellcat ever undertaken. The Lone Star Flight Museum's F6F-5 was originally assigned Bureau Number 94204 and was accepted by the Navy on 27 July 1945, delivery to Naval Air Station San Diego, California, being made on 1 August. Its operational

Above: The F6F Hellcat formates with its older brother the Grumman F4F Wildcat. Both aircraft are owned by the Lone Star Flight Museum of Galveston, Texas. (Brian Silcox)

career was short since it was immediately sent into storage at NAS Santa Ana, California. In October 1947 it was flown to NAS Alameda, California, for modification and thirteen days later was flown back to NAS Santa Ana for storage. Removed from storage in December 1951, the aircraft was transferred to NAS Willow Grove, Pennsylvania, but less than a month later it was moved back to NAS Alameda, where it served until January 1953.

The new year brought a flurry of activity to BuNo 94204. It went to NAS

Oakland, California, then cross-country to NAS Willow Grove in January. In May it was flown to NAS Norfolk, Virginia, and back to NAS Oakland. In August 1954 the Hellcat was placed back in storage at NAS San Diego with only 603 flight hours on the airframe, the engine having been overhauled at 300 hours. On 9 July 1957 all remaining F6F-5 and F6F-5K aircraft in storage were declared surplus and designated for sale as scrap or flying aircraft.

BuNo 94204's civilian career began in 1959 when the aircraft was purchased by the Normandie Iron and Metal Company from the Navy at San Diego's North Island. Ed Maloney, founder of the Planes of Fame Museum, Chino, California, bought this and a sister ship for his collec-

tion. He later traded 94204 to Eddie Fisher for his German Me 262, which is now on display at the Planes of Fame. Fisher did not fly the aircraft and it was purchased by Mike Coutches in May 1970. In the late 1950s and early 1960s Coutches rescued many rare warbirds. He flew the F6F to his base of operations at the Hayward Air Terminal, south of Oakland, and in October 1974 he flew it to the Wagons to Wings Museum at the Flying Lady Restaurant in Morgan Hill, California. The Hellcat was displayed here until 1986, when it was purchased by the Lone Star Flight Museum, of Galveston, Texas.

In October 1986 Steve Picatti, a warbird restoration specialist based at the Hayward Air Terminal, and five em-

Left: The Hellcat's fuselage has been mated with the centre-section and the engine firewall forward has been installed. The restoration is making progress. (Nicholas Veronico)

Below: The Hellcat is starting to look like an aeroplane. The cockpit restoration and the addition of the second seat are under way. (Nicholas Veronico)

ployees began working full time to restore the F6F. Picatti and his crew travelled south to the Wagons to Wings Museum to dismantle the F6F for the trip back to Hayward by road. Originally the plan was to install a new engine, inspect and repair any 'squawks' and prepare the Hellcat for the ferry flight to the Lone Star Flight Museum. However, Lone Star founder Robert Waltrip visited Hayward to inspect the work already performed.

Although he was satisfied, he said he would be feel safer if the aircraft had new fuel tanks. 'So I started on the fuel tanks, but to get to the tanks you have to remove the entire cockpit,' says Picatti. 'Mr Waltrip came out and asked, "Why don't you do the whole aircraft?" Well, his idea of restoring the whole aircraft is unlike any other restoration you've ever seen! It has to be new, or better than new. We took the whole centre section off the fuselage –

completely de-mated it. Everything that could come apart has been apart and all the pieces have been magnafluxed, subjected to eddy currents or zyglowed (nondestructive testing). So it has now been completely inspected.'

The entire aircraft has been de-skinned, stripped and primed and then repainted. A&P's Cliff Lofthouse and Andy Macfie were responsible for stripping the aircraft, de-mating the fuselage from the wing and then beginning the rebuilding process. The only corrosion found was on the right cockpit wall where the heater duct vented to the exterior. Picatti said that the corrosion was so minimal because there is no dissimilar metal contact in the Hellcat airframe. When Grumman built the F6Fs, all surfaces on the airframe were painted and then assembled. 'We stayed with Grumman's specifications and then went one step further,' explains Picatti. 'We started with an etch primer that adheres to bare metal, then we put a palomide primer over the top of that. Then, to get a better and smoother final coat, we put an epoxy primer over the palomide primer. It takes longer to dry, but it's harder. We then spray the finishing coat on top of that. That's the way the Hellcat was built from scratch.'

Prior to its reinstallation on the airframe, the Hellcat's Pratt & Whitney R-2800 was overhauled by Keith Dayton Engines of Livermore, California. Now, when the cowlings and access panels are off, many parts look as if they have been chrome plated, but they have not. What you see is polish. After the oxygen system was reinstalled, the hydraulic system was

replumbed. The old hydraulic lines were removed – all 130 – and new ones bent, inspected and anodized and then re-installed in the aircraft. Another major hurdle was the rigging of the landing gear. The Hellcat's gear retracts just like a Curtiss P-40's, the leg swinging backwards and the wheel and tyre rotating through ninety degrees to fit flush into the wing, inboard of the wing folding mechanism.

Once Picatti was satisfied with the gear operation, he and his crew turned their attention to the three major modifications that were to be made to the F6F – the installation of a second seat, complete rewiring, and the modernization of the cockpit. During wartime, the area behind the pilot's seat was occupied by vacuum-

Below: The rear fuselage receives a coat of primer. The cockpit windscreen has been installed. (Nicholas Veronico)

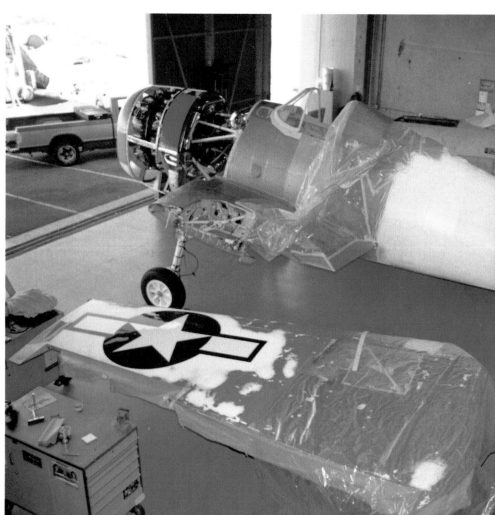

tube radios, but with today's solid state electronics this area was left empty. The Lone Star Museum directed Picatti to install a second seat. Franz Traeg was responsible for much of the sheet metal work, including the installation of the second seat and its canopy. All of the Hellcat's wiring was replaced with non-toxic conduit leading to junction boxes, with cannon plugs for ease of maintenance. Jose Parenas single-handedly rewired the entire electrical system, a modification which went hand in hand with the modernization of the cockpit. New, updated instrumentation and radios will make this Hellcat fully IFR-certified.

The Lone Star Museum instructed Picatti to restore the Hellcat in Commander Alex Vraciu's VF-16 *Airedales* markings. Vraciu, who coincidentally lives not far from the Picatti shop, is the Navy's fourth leading ace with nineteen confirmed kills. He was a visitor many times while the restoration was in progress.

Vraciu earned his wings in August 1942. His first operational posting was with Lieutenant-Commander Edward H. ('Butch') O'Hare's Fighting Squadron Three, VF-3 (later Fighting Six, VF-6). Vraciu's element of the squadron flew with O'Hare from the aircraft carrier USS *Independence* and 5 October 1943 saw the first demonstration of (then Lieutenant) Vraciu's deadly marksmanship. While flying combat air patrol as section leader to 'Butch' O'Hare, he shot down a 'Zeke' (the Allied code-name for the Mitsubishi A6M, more commonly known as the Zero) and destroyed another 'Zeke' and a twin-engine 'Betty' bomber on the ground. In addition to his aerial victories, Vraciu

Left: A jubilant Lieutenant Vraciu holds up six fingers, representing the gaggle of 'Judy' dive-bombers destroyed in one sortie during the 'Marianas Turkey Shoot'. Vraciu knocked the six aircraft out of the air in about eight minutes. (Via Alex Vraciu)

would eventually destroy a total of 21 aircraft on the ground. On 20 November 1943 he downed a 'Betty' over the island of Tarawa. That same evening the *Independence* was torpedoed and his squadron was then transferred to the USS *Intrepid*.

At this point in his career Vraciu had accumulated only 720.2 flying hours. After a flight over Roi Airfield, on Kwajalein Island, on 29 January 1944, he qualified as an 'ace', downing three 'Bettys'. February 16 saw Vraciu's guns account for three 'Zekes' and a single-engine 'Rufe' seaplane, all of which fell into the sea near Truk. His total was now nine enemy aircraft destroyed in the air. The *Intrepid* was torpedoed during the night of the 16th. Air Group Six was then transferred back to the United States and Lieutenant

(JG) Vraciu requested and received a transfer to Fighting Sixteen (VF-16).

Back out in the action on board the USS *Lexington*, Vraciu got two more 'Zekes' over the Truk Islands on 29 April. The total was now eleven. On 12 June 1944, in the face of intense anti-aircraft fire, he sank a 6,500-ton Japanese cargo ship in Tanapag Harbor, Saipan, with a direct hit on the stern. Two days later he was returning from an escort mission when he saw a lone 'Betty' reconnaissance bomber north of Saipan near Medihilla Island at 18,000 feet, which he downed. Five days later, on 19 June, Vraciu and his wingman took off from their carrier but could not keep up with their squadron leader. The latter had just had a new engine installed and 'his own

Below: Hooking up the power prior to the first engine run. (Nicholas Veronico)
Below right: The Grumman fighter's R-2800 swings the propeller prior to start-up. (Nicholas Veronico)

wingman's engine froze trying to keep up with him. He ditched in the water and they picked him up the next day,' recalls Vraciu. Vraciu could not shift his engine into high blower, and so he could not reach the assigned patrol altitude. He was instructed to orbit over his carrier and then vectored towards a flight of single-engine Yokosuka 'Judy' dive bombers.

This day was to become known as the 'Marianas Turkey Shoot'. Vraciu tells the story of his six kills in eight minutes: 'We ran into a batch of 'em. Forty or fifty of 'em – a rambling mass. Sure enough, there they were, about 2,000 or 3,000 feet below. I started to go down and another Hellcat had designs on the same Judy I was going after, so I aborted my run to keep from colliding with him. I then pulled back up.

'I had an old bird and I had oil all over the windshield. Our purpose was to keep them together – we knew if they started to separate, the torpedo planes would go down below and the dive bombers would pick their targets. I then started after another Judy on the formation's edge. I got him and he started down in flames. I pulled up, coming from the rear and saw two in a loose wing formation. I got the rear one, moved up, dipped the wing and then got the next one. Number four seemed to be breaking formation. I worked in real close and got a short burst to the wing root. He caught fire and went down.

'I saw a group of three Judys beginning to make their dive-bombing run. I got the tail-ender in the wing root. The next Judy was about one-fifth of the way down in his dive. I must have hit his bomb, as he blew up in a big explosion. I started for the last one, but he ran into a solid wall of steel thrown up from the

Fly Past, Fly Present

battleship below. I looked around and saw nothing but Hellcats in the sky. Glancing backwards, all I could see was a 35-mile long pattern of flaming oil slicks in the water.'

Vraciu had shot down six 'Judys' in eight minutes using only 360 rounds of the 2,400 on board! The next day's retaliatory strike (20 June) against the Japanese fleet saw Vraciu get his nineteenth kill, a 'Zeke'.

Many feel that Vraciu's actions on these four missions from 12 to 19 June – eight aircraft confirmed destroyed, six on a single hop, plus a 6,500 ton cargo ship sunk – should have earned him the Medal

Grumman F6F-5

Wing span: (Spread) 43ft 10in (13.36m), (folded) 16ft 2in (4.93m)
Length: 33ft 10in (10.31m)
Height: 14ft 5in (4.39m) over propeller
Speed: Maximum 392mph (631kph), stall 79mph (127kph) with power off
Armament: Six .50-calibre machine guns plus 2,000lb (907kg) of bombs or six 5in high-velocity aerial rockets
Powerplant: One Pratt & Whitney R-2800-10W (water injected) capable of 2,000hp at 2,700rpm (take-off) and 1,550hp at 2,550rpm (21,500ft)

Below: The Hellcat ready for its first engine run after its three-year restoration. (Nicholas Veronico)

Below: The finished Hellcat, looking better than on the day it was completed by Grumman. (Nicholas Veronico)

of Honor. He was indeed recommended for the medal, but his recommendation, dated 26 June and signed by Lieutenant-Commander R. C. Gillette USN, was 'lost'. Subsequent attempts by members of the public to get the Navy to award him the medal have fallen on the deaf ears of bureaucrats who fail to recognize Vraciu's bravery.

Vraciu was the Navy's leading ace for four months during 1944. However, on a strafing run in the Clark Field area of the Philippines he was 'potted' by anti-aircraft fire. Forced to bail out, he landed and fought against the Japanese with the Philippines guerrillas. In 1957, when Com-

mander Vraciu was the Commanding Officer of VF-51, he won the High Individual Air-to-Air competition at the Naval Air Weapons Meet in El Centro, California, flying a North American FJ Fury jet. He was one of the Navy's first 'Top Guns'. On the preserved Hellcat, the markings of ace Alex Vraciu were applied by hand by aviation artist Skip Raines over the Navy tri-colour scheme which was painted by Mike Picatti.

'It's as new as when it came from the factory – in fact a little bit better, I think,' Picatti says of the Hellcat restoration. The Lone Star Flight Museum maintains the F6F in flyable condition at

Fly Past, Fly Present

its Galveston, Texas, facility. It resides in outstanding company with the museum's fleet of restored vintage aircraft, which include a flying P-38 Lightning, a B-17G and a razor-back P-47G Thunderbolt.

The Saving of Swordfish W5856

Although the Fairey Swordfish – affectionately known as the 'Stringbag' – originated in the early 1930s and was obsolete by the time it entered service with the Royal Navy, this famous biplane torpedo bomber served with distinction throughout the Second World War. More than 2,000 examples were built; surprisingly, the majority (1,660) were constructed by Blackburn at their Sherburn-in-Elmet factory near Leeds. The illustrious 'Stringbag' outlived its intended replacement, the Fairey Albacore, and was the last biplane to see active service.

Swordfish W5856 was one such aircraft, completed as part of a batch of 100 Mk IIs and flying for the first time from Sherburn on 21 October 1941, Trafalgar Day. The aircraft was delivered to Gibraltar on board the SS *Empire Morn* and joined the Mediterranean Fleet for approximately one year, following which it was returned to Britain for refurbishment at Fairey's Stockport factory. W5856 flew once again on 4 February 1943 and was then delivered to No 9 Pilot Advanced Flying Unit RAF at Errol in Perthshire. As part of C Flight the aircraft was used for training purposes, sorties being flown from Crail, generally over the Firth of Forth.

During February 1944 the aircraft was transferred to Manston for a series of

tactical trials over the English Channel and then returned to Errol, where a take-off accident, due to power failure, resulted in the aircraft's being withdrawn from use. After being dismantled and transported to Hamble, it was crated and shipped to Canada, where it entered service with the Royal Canadian Air Force, joining No 1 Naval Air Gunners' School at Yarmouth in Nova Scotia.

With the end of the war in sight, No 1 NAGS disbanded on 13 March 1945 and W5856 was handed over to the War Assets Commission and placed in storage at Mount Hope in Ontario, having been declared APDAL (Aircraft Pending Disposal). Eventually the aircraft was sold on the civilian market, and in response to an advertisement in a trade magazine Sir William Roberts purchased it from an English businessman in Texas and transported the dismantled airframe back to Perthshire to join the Strathallan Collection in July 1977.

After arriving in Scotland the airframe was scheduled to undergo extensive restoration, but although some work was initiated – largely on the mainplanes, the rear fuselage and the engine – the Strathallan Collection was dispersed to various buyers before it could be completed. British Aerospace, in association with the Royal Navy and Rolls-Royce, formed the Swordfish Heritage Trust and agreed to undertake a complete restoration.

Left, upper: The Lone Star Flight Museum's Hellcat in its element. (Brian Silcox)
Left: Swordfish W5658 high over British Aerospace's Brough factory, the Humber estuary in the background. (BAe)

On 13 December 1990 the aircraft was transported to British Aerospace's (formerly Blackburn's) factory at Brough in Yorkshire in two curtain-sided trucks, arriving late the following day. The fuselage, wings, engine and smaller components were unloaded two days later for preliminary examination. The fuselage and wing structure appeared to be in reasonable condition, no doubt as a result of the attention received from the restoration personnel at Strathallan. However, the engine exhaust ring, aircraft switches and pipework were all found to be severely corroded.

Following the arrival of W5856 at Brough, Graham Chisnall, BAe Brough's Chief Engineer, was appointed head of the restoration project and Graham Duck, John Owens, Peter Hatch and Trevor Brewin joined the team; other key personnel with experience in design, structures, instrumentation, aerodynamics and non-destructive testing were also asked to participate in the undertaking at various stages. The team did not set a completion date for the restoration, and it was only after a detailed structural survey of the aircraft that some idea of the amount of work required was established.

The project was essentially a part-time venture, although three engineers were assigned full time. In the twenty-eight months it took to complete the restoration, there were periods, sometimes lasting up to three months, during which nobody worked on the aircraft, owing to requirements elsewhere within the factory, which naturally took priority. Regular team meetings were held to discuss

Fly Past, Fly Present

the work, many of the specialists being part-time participants who would otherwise be unaware how it was progressing. Open discussion was crucial as there was an ever-present need to ensure that the individual elements of the restoration would all come together at the same time: it was acknowledged that there would be little point in completing 99 per cent of the restoration, for example, if one other small component was going to require another six months of work.

The initial structural survey was conducted carefully and in painstaking detail by the British Aerospace team. Various non-destructive testing techniques were employed, for example x-rays, eddy currents, magnetic flaw detection and ultrasonics, establishing the complete structural integrity of each airframe com-

Below: An early view of the Swordfish restoration project, illustrating the main components at Brough following their delivery from Strathallan. (BAe)
Right, upper: The port lower wing, showing the intricate internal construction. (BAe)
Right, lower: The main fuselage section, showing some of the careful restoration work undertaken by the team at Brough. (BAe)

ponent. BAe's Design and Structures departments assessed what repairs would be appropriate for each item. The Royal Navy's Historic Flight at Yeovilton was the first point of contact for the supply of equipment such as instrumentation. Other manufactured items were obtained from specialist suppliers, and many companies furnished materials and components free of charge. The Imperial War Museum at Duxford also supplied some

components, taken from its own non-airworthy Swordfish, in exchange for items removed from W5856.

The Pegasus engine was taken to Rolls-Royce's factory at Filton for complete refurbishment. Although it is not known whether the engine was W5856's original Pegasus, it is now attached to LS326, the second (original) Swordfish operated by the Historic Flight. The engines from both aircraft were refurbished almost simultaneously, but LS326's was the first to be completed, prompting the decision to deliver it to Brough in order to allow W5856 to fly at the earliest opportunity.

The refurbishment complete, W5856 made a successful ground run on 22 April 1993, and on 12 May the aircraft taxied on to Brough's runway and, after a predictably short take-off run, rose effortlessly into the air. The first post-restoration flight took place some ten days before the aircraft was officially handed over to the Royal Navy during BAe Brough's Families' Day, when some 40,000 people visited the factory to see the newly restored Swordfish. The test flight lasted about fifty minutes, and despite one or two minor problems the pilot pronounced himself very pleased with the aircraft's performance. The Swordfish's braking system features a bag containing compressed air to which the wheel brake drums are applied, and on this first flight there was a significant loss of air which resulted in some braking difficulties, but the problem was quickly rectified by the team. The aircraft's compass was also defective, but was noted as a deferred item in the log book prior to flight. Brough is an

Fly Past, Fly Present

unsuitable location for compass-swing alignment thanks to the high metallic content of the airfield's soil and the adjustment was later made at Yeovilton. A couple of other instruments also needed attention, but there were no real problems at this stage and the restoration team were delighted with the results of the flight, not least because it had taken place ahead of the self-imposed deadline, 22 May, which had been set some five months previously.

Having joined the Historic Flight, W5856 is now subject to the same flying restrictions as the Flight's other Swordfish. Flying is limited to fifty hours a year, chiefly to preserve the life of the engine, although no date has been fixed for the retirement of either airframe. Both are flown fairly gently, and normally only in the spring and summer, in reasonable weather, in order to minimize the possibility of damaging them. British Aerospace has not imposed any physical limitations on W5856, but the Royal Navy restricts manoeuvres to +2g/–0g and a maximum angle of bank of 60°. The maximum speed is 130 knots and the ceiling 10,000 feet, although, as one might imagine, this altitude is unlikely to be reached very often in any case!

It is difficult to establish just how many people were involved, directly or indirectly, with the Swordfish project, as Graham Duck explains: 'I wouldn't even like to guess just how many personnel got involved throughout the factory. The core team included people with many, many years of experience on projects such as the Buccaneer and the Phantom, both here and at our former site at Holme-on-

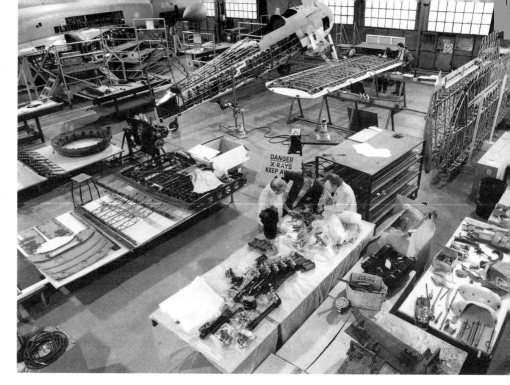

Left, upper: The Sword-fish seen during the reconstruction process. (BAe)
Left, lower: The huge underslung torpedo, taken from LS326. (BAe)
***Below:** Also borrowed from the Historic Flight's original Swordfish was the newly restored Pegasus engine. (BAe)*

Spalding Moor. Our design engineer just missed the Swordfish production line, starting work here at Brough just a few years after production of the Swordfish had ended at Sherburn-in-Elmet. We did make contact with people who had worked on the original Swordfish production lines. I recall one lady in her nineties who used to sew the fabric-covered bags for the wing sections, and we tracked down other people too.'

Duck continues: 'One of the main problems we faced when we began the project was a lack of design information. Being such an old aircraft, we had a hard time recovering information, particularly the drawings. After consulting the His-

toric Flight I discovered that RAF Hendon did have a large amount of information on Fairey Aviation, including some drawings. We found over a hundred drawings on microfilm, and they were transferred on to paper, but they weren't of any great use to us. We were looking for some assembly drawings and we didn't find enough of these to help us to any great extent. However, the Swordfish Air Publications were made available to us by the Historic Flight, and one item which we did find very useful was Air Publication 15-17, Volume 1, which in its October 1937 second edition was entitled *The Swordfish Aeroplane. Torpedo, Spotting, Reconnaissance, Land, Ship or Float Seaplane. Pegasus Three Engine*, issued by the Air Ministry. This was a very useful manual from which our engineers and design and structures people could glean information.'

In terms of instrumentation and equipment, it was accepted that some changes to the original Swordfish specification would have to be made, to enable the Royal Navy to operate and maintain the aircraft. In particular, the electrical system was altered to 24 volts, the original 12-volt system being insupportable in respect of spares, and a generator taken from a De Havilland Devon was installed. Maintainability also dictated the cockpit layout, as many of the original instruments would have been impossible to service. BAe decided to match W5856's layout as closely as possible to that of LS326 in order to aid pilot familiarity, and there is a fairly good supply of instruments available from the Historic Flight. Consequently, the rpm indicator was taken from

Fly Past, Fly Present

a Devon, the engine temperature system from a Sea Hawk and the oil pressure indicator from a Chipmunk, adapted to interface with the original Swordfish systems.

The lack of original reference material caused the restoration team many problems, and constant comparisons with surviving Swordfish airframes were necessary, as Graham Duck explains: 'Because Yeovilton is so far away from us at Brough, we couldn't always send the team down there to look at LS326. So, some six months into the project, we found that the Navy had another Swordfish at Lee-on-Solent, which was on permanent static display. We concluded that it was in reasonable condition and arranged with the Navy to transport the aircraft up to Brough. It took two days to get the Swordfish up here, and it stood next to W5856 to act as a reference guide for the engineers. We started with boxes of components, and although we knew what the aircraft

Below: A beautiful photograph of a beautiful aeroplane, clearly illustrating the freshly applied fabric covering to the wings and tail. (BAe)

looked like we didn't know if we had all the right components, or if items varied between different Swordfish variants. We needed as much information as possible, and Swordfish NF389 really helped us along.'

Much of the original structure was retained in the restoration, although some items had to be rebuilt. Some eighty per cent of the tailplane was manufactured from scratch, together with smaller items such as flying control pulleys, and some of the main tubular structure of the fuselage and the entire electrical system were replaced. However, most of the aircraft was in reasonably sound condition and did not require replacing. The wing spars were of major concern, and until the team took delivery of the wings it did not know what to expect. Had the team been forced to re-manufacture the wing spars, the project's completion date would have slipped considerably. However, after a thorough x-ray and video-probe examination, it was found that there was no

significant corrosion. Some minor repairs were made to various parts of the wing, to strengthen the spars locally where corrosion had caused damage, and the team's engineers made new toolings to produce channels to fit over the existing spars. The team also had to ensure that minor areas of corrosion were completely inactive, in order to avoid problems in the future.

Of course, the Swordfish's fabric covering also needed to be replaced, as Graham Duck recalls: 'Fabric covering has really died out within the aerospace industry, and we certainly don't do that kind of thing at Brough. It's only smaller components on light aircraft which still use this kind of construction. Some companies still specialize in fabric covering, and we made contact with a local company near York, and some of the smaller components and removable panels were transported to their workshops for completion. But for the larger items like the wings we had to cover them on site, and

Below: The completed Swordfish, with BAe's logo just visible on the rudder. (BAe)

we had to take over the airfield fire station while we completed this task. It's a complicated and time-consuming task, and first off you have to cover all the surface hard points with a tape. Things like rivets have to be covered, and then the internal wing ribs and stringers are covered with a woven material. Then you place what is basically a fabric bag over the wing. The bag is then stitched into place, and once it's tightly in place it is covered with three layers of dope, followed by a final coat. We had four wings to do, and then the fuselage too – all completed in the fire station, out on the apron next to the main operations hangar.'

The Swordfish was then painted in pre-Second World War colours, the scheme having been selected by the Royal Navy to represent an aircraft flown by Captain Nigel Skene, Royal Marines, in 1939 during a series of summer exercises. Skene was the Commanding Officer of 810 TSR (Torpedo, Spotting and Reconnaissance) Squadron, later being awarded a DFC after leading the squadron during operations off the Norwegian coast. The scheme is essentially silver, on to which the red and blue colours of HMS *Ark Royal* have been applied (810 NAS was operating from the carrier in 1939) around the rear fuselage. The yellow fuselage stripe

Right: A glorious in-flight photograph of the recently restored Swordfish W5856 passing over the Humber Bridge shortly before the aircraft's handover to the Royal Navy Historic Flight. (BAe)

Left: A mid-restoration view, emphasizing the sturdy nature of the Swordfish's undercarriage, which was designed to withstand heavy deck landings. (BAe)

was applied specifically for an exercise, identifying 810 (TSR) NAS as 'Yellow Squadron' during the event. Black 'no step' stripes are applied to the upper fuselage and wing surfaces, and smaller 'no step' areas are outlined in Buffer's Pink. Non-authentic markings are confined to the rear fuselage, where 'Royal Navy' titles have been applied below the tailplane, while small BAe logos have been attached to the rudder, in recognition of the outstanding restoration task performed by the British Aerospace team.

W5856 enjoys the distinction of being the oldest surviving example of the Fairey Swordfish and has now settled into its new home at Yeovilton in company with long-term resident LS326. Both aircraft are available for air show appearances around the country, individually and, less frequently, as an exciting two-aircraft display. Who would have thought that, in the mid-1990s, two 'Stringbags' would be in the air together again? As for the BAe restoration team, no decisions have been made concerning possible future projects, although it is quite likely that another aircraft will be restored following the success of the first. There is absolutely no hint as to what the subject might be, but one could be forgiven for imagining an even more ambitious plan. Nobody needs reminding that Brough was the home of the Blackburn Buccaneer!

Keeping the Show on the Road

Peter Jacobs/Nicholas Veronico

Each year thousands of enthusiasts travel to see the Battle of Britain Memorial Flight, either performing at air displays or reposing at its home base at RAF Coningsby. It continues to serve as a living reminder of those airmen who gave their lives in defence of their country.

First known as the Historic Aircraft Flight, the BBMF was formed at Biggin Hill in 1957. It originally consisted of three Supermarine Spitfire Mk XIXs and a Hawker Hurricane Mk IIC but was expanded later that year to include two Spitfire Mk XVIs. When Biggin Hill was closed to operational flying the following year, the Flight moved to North Weald, and then to Martlesham Heath in May 1958. In 1961 the Flight moved again, this time to Horsham St Faith, but by now it was struggling to survive. Both the Spitfire Mk XVIs had been lost in accidents and two of the Mk XIXs had been transferred to perform 'gate guardian' duties, leaving just PM631 and the faithful Hurricane LF363. However, the importance of maintaining such a flight was realized, and when Horsham St Faith was closed in

1963 the two aircraft were moved to Coltishall and things began to improve.

By 1972 the number of Spitfires had risen to four with the return of a Mk XIX (PS853) and the addition of a Mk VB (AB910) and a Mk IIA (P7350). However, there was still just the single Hurricane. Recognizing the needs of the Flight, Hawkers refurbished the last Hurricane to come off the production line, PZ865, and presented it to the Flight in 1972. Avro Lancaster PA474 joined the Flight the following year and the new title 'Battle of Britain Memorial Flight' was adopted. Three years later, in 1976, the Flight moved to Coningsby, where it remains today.

In 1985 the BBMF was allocated a De Havilland Devon (VP981) for training and support duties and two years later one of the founder aircraft, Spitfire Mk XIX PS915, was refurbished and re-joined the Flight. Sadly, in 1991 the original Hurri-

Right: RAF Coningsby has been home to the Battle of Britain Memorial Flight since 1976. Here the famous three – Spitfire (bottom), Hurricane and Lancaster – are pictured in 1990. (Sergeant Rick Brewell)

cane crash-landed at Wittering after suffering a major engine malfunction. However, it is hoped that the aircraft will eventually be rebuilt. The Flight also possesses a Chipmunk trainer (WK518), which is used for a variety of purposes ranging from initial and continuation training for the fighter pilots to the ferrying of support personnel and spares. The most recent addition is a Dakota C Mk 3 (ZA947), which arrived from Farnborough in 1993. A sixth Spitfire, Mk XIX MK356, is currently being refurbished at St Athan and will join the Flight in 1996, bringing the total number of aircraft on strength to twelve.

The BBMF is currently commanded by Squadron Leader Andy Tomalin. An experienced Qualified Flying Instructor, he had accumulated 6,800 flying hours during his 32 years of service with the RAF. His operational flying was on Victor tankers and he saw service during the Falklands War of 1982. During the display season he is the Captain of the Lancaster. 'It is undoubtedly a high point in my career to be able to fly the Lancaster,' he says. 'Although it is hard work, it is very gratifying and a great privilege to command one of the RAF's major flying display teams.'

As Officer Commanding, Squadron Leader Tomalin is the only full-time aircrew member of the Flight. He currently has a warrant officer, an engineering team and two administrators under his command, the remaining aircrew all being volunteers who serve other full-time appointments in the RAF. 'My role as Officer Commanding is more than just flying old aircraft,' he continues. 'It is very

much a time-consuming and complex planning task in putting the season together and then making sure that things run as smoothly as possible once the season has begun.' Throughout the year he is continuously involved in hosting visits, giving presentations and lectures and helping to deal with the numerous enquiries which occur daily – all part of being OC BBMF!

P7350 is the oldest airworthy Spitfire in the world and the oldest aircraft in the Flight, having entered service in August 1940. A Mk IIA, it served with Nos 266, 603, 616 and 64 Squadrons and is the only aircraft in the BBMF to have seen operational service during the Battle of Britain

Left: OC BBMF Squadron Leader Andy Tomalin at the controls of the Lancaster. (David Muscroft)

Below: PS853 is one of the BBMF's three Spitfire Mk XIXs and was one of the founder members of the Flight in 1957. (Jeremy Flack)

itself, flying with Nos 266 and 603 Squadrons from Hornchurch. Pilots flying P7350 shot down three enemy aircraft, although the Spitfire did suffer damage in combat. After the war it was sold as scrap but was later presented to the museum at RAF Colerne. In 1967 it was restored to airworthiness and registered G-AWIJ for the filming of The Battle of Britain. The aircraft joined the BBMF in 1968.

Spitfire Mk VB AB910 was delivered to the RAF in August 1941 and saw service with Nos 222, 130, 133, 242, 416, 402 and 527 Squadrons. At Hibaldstow LACW Margaret Horton took to the air while sitting on the tail of this aircraft, the pilot completely unaware of her presence. Fortunately, the latter quickly noticed that the handling of the aircraft was far from normal and landed after one quick circuit! In November 1947 this Spitfire was registered G-AISU for air racing but in 1953 was returned to Vickers following a

heavy landing. In 1965 it was flown to RAF Coltishall and presented to the Flight.

Mk XIX PS853 was delivered to the RAF in January 1945 and saw service with No 1 Photographic Reconnaissance Unit, No 34 Support Unit and No 16 Squadron before the end of hostilities. After the war the aircraft was assigned to the Temperature and Humidity Monitoring Flight (THUM) at Woodvale. In 1957 PS853 became one of the founder members of the BBMF but was moved to West Raynham for gate guardian duties in 1958, returning to the Flight in 1964.

PS915, a Spitfire XIX, entered service in June 1945 and took part in photographic reconnaissance development trials. After serving with No 2 Squadron in Europe, the aircraft spent time with No 9 Maintenance Unit before joining THUM at Woodvale in 1954. It was one of the Flight's original Spitfires but was quickly

transferred to gate guardian duties at West Malling, Leuchars and Brawdy. Subsequently refurbished to airworthy condition, PS915 was returned to the Flight in 1987.

The only Spitfire in the BBMF not to have seen war service is the Mk XIX PM631, which was delivered to the RAF in November 1945. The aircraft was modified for meteorological work in 1950 and became part of THUM at Hooton Park and Woodvale. It was one of the founder members of the Flight in 1957 and is the BBMF's longest-serving Spitfire.

LF363, a Hurricane Mk IIC, is believed to be the last Hurricane to have entered service, having been delivered to No 5 Maintenance Unit in January 1944. Before the war ended the aircraft saw operational service with Nos 63, 309 and 267 Squadrons. This was the Hurricane which formed part of the original Flight in 1957. The aircraft was severely damaged in its crash-landing on 11 September

Above: PZ865 is now the Flight's only airworthy Hurricane. It was the last of 14,533 Hurricanes to be built. (Philip Makanna)

1991 (although, fortunately, the pilot was not seriously injured) but will probably be rebuilt.

A total of 14,533 Hurricanes were built, and the Mk IIC PZ865 was the last, rolling off the production line in July 1944. It never saw service with the RAF, having been immediately bought back from the Air Ministry by Hawkers for use as a test and communications aircraft. Registered G-AMAU, it took part in several air races and finished second in the

1950 King's Cup Air Race. PZ865's film roles have included Angels One-Five and Reach for the Sky. Recognizing the needs of the Flight for a second Hurricane, Hawkers refurbished the aircraft and presented it to the Flight in 1972.

Only five pilots are fortunate enough to fly the Flight's fighters during the display season. Training an already experienced RAF jet fighter pilot to fly the Spitfire and Hurricane is not a simple task and it takes time for him to gain experience. Two of the pilots get the opportunity to fly the Spitfire and Hurricane by virtue of their senior executive appointments at RAF Coningsby: the station is currently home to three Tornado F.3 fighter squadrons and traditionally the Station Commander (when a pilot, as opposed to a navigator) is included as one of the five pilots, as is the Officer Commanding Operations Wing. However, these senior appointments tend to be short-term and the Station Commander and OC Ops Wing are lucky to get two full display seasons. The three remaining pilots are currently all experienced Tornado F.3 instructors serving with No 56 Squadron at Coningsby and all have been displaying the BBMF fighters for several years. These pilots have traditionally been selected from instructors at Coningsby: pilot availability during the display season tends to be better from the training unit than from the operational squadrons.

Regular display pilots Squadron Leaders Allan Martin and Chris Stevens began their operational careers on the Lightning and are now Tornado F.3 instructors with well over 5,000 hours of flying behind them. However, the most experienced fighter pilot on the Flight is Squadron Leader Paul ('Major') Day, who, as Fighter Leader, is responsible for training the newly selected fighter pilots and for continuation training between the display seasons. Day's career is impressive. Having joined the RAF in 1961 he flew Hunters between 1963 and 1971, during which time he served in the Far East with No 20 Squadron (1964–66), the United Kingdom with Nos 54, 79 and 63 Squadrons (1966–68) and the Middle East with

No 208 Squadron (1968–71). He converted to the Phantom in 1971 and completed further operational tours with No 14 Squadron in Germany (1971–74) and on exchange with the US Air Force at Luke Air Force Base (1975–78). On his return home he served as an instructor with No 228 OCU from 1978 to 1987, joining the BBMF as a display pilot in 1980. In 1988 he converted to the Tornado F.3 and served as an instructor with No 229 OCU and later No 56 Squadron, with which unit he serves today. He has accumulated a staggering 2,000 hours on Hunters, over 3,000 on Phantoms and more than 1,000 on Tor-

Below: PA474 outside the BBMF hangar at RAF Coningsby. The hangar and Visitors' Centre are open to the public throughout the year (BBMF)

nados, plus a further 1,000 on the Spitfire and Hurricane. BBMF Fighter Leader since 1982, Day was awarded the Air Force Cross in 1988 for his services to air combat training.

Initial training is carried out on the Flight's Chipmunk. It may have been many years since an RAF pilot flew a single-engine, propeller-driven aircraft and so it is necessary for him to re-familiarize himself with the very basic flying controls and handling characteristics of the aeroplane. The Chipmunk does have some things in common with the Spitfire and Hurricane – it is, for exam-

ple, a 'tail dragger', and the art of taxying, taking off and landing is somewhat different from that practised in a Tornado. Having completed some 25 hours of Chipmunk flying, the pilot progresses to the Harvard at Boscombe Down to gain experience in a higher-speed and better performing aircraft. Only a few trips are made in the Harvard before the pilot is cleared to fly the Hurricane, whereupon he gains as much experience as possible on this aircraft before getting the opportunity to fly the Spitfire. Because the BBMF operates three marks of the Spitfire, all with differing handling charac-

teristics, time is spent and experience gained on the Mk II before the Mk V and finally the more powerful Mk XIX are tackled.

Of the 7,377 Lancasters built, PA474 is just one of two surviving airworthy examples (the other being in Canada). Built in 1945, this particular aircraft was intended for operations in the Far East, but the war with Japan ended before it could take part in hostilities and it was later assigned to No 82 Squadron for photo-reconnaissance duties in East and South Africa. Having later served with Flight Refuelling Ltd and the College of Aeronautics at Cranfield, PA474 was adopted by the Air Historical Branch and moved to RAF Henlow in preparation for its display at the RAF Museum at Hendon. However, the Commanding Officer of No 44 Squadron gained permission for the aircraft to be transferred to RAF Waddington and, following a lengthy restoration at

that station, the aircraft was allowed to fly once more in 1967 and it joined the Flight in November 1973. Dubbed *The City of Lincoln*, the Lancaster carries the coat of arms of the city on the forward fuselage in recognition of the long and deep association of the Lancaster, and of Bomber Command, with the city and county.

During a display the Lancaster is crewed by two pilots, a navigator and an air engineer. As OC BBMF, Squadron Leader Andy Tomalin captains the Lancaster during its displays. There are generally two pilots at Coningsby who are qualified as co-pilots for the displays, each taking his turn during the season. Three navigators qualified on the aircraft are available during the season and these are selected from instructors serving with No 56 Squadron. The task of the navigator can be very demanding as is it his responsibility to ensure that the Lancaster (and

Below: The latest addition to the Flight is a Dakota C Mk 3, seen here on approach to Gibraltar in 1993. (RAF Gibraltar)

the fighters if these are in formation) is in the right place at exactly the right time. The fourth member of the crew, the air engineer, is one of three selected from the instructors at the Air Engineer School at RAF Finningley.

Dakota C Mk 3 ZA947 was manufactured in February 1942 and began its flying career with the US Army Air Corps. It was transferred to the Royal Canadian Air Force in September 1943 and later served in Europe. The RCAF declared the aircraft surplus to requirements in 1971 and it became part of the Royal Aircraft Establishment at Farnborough, adopting the serial number KG661. The RAE used it for a variety of trials, ranging from the

dropping of sonobuoys to acting as a launch platform for remotely piloted vehicles. Doubts were raised as to the aircraft's true identity in 1978 when documentary evidence was produced to show that the original KG661 had been destroyed in 1944, and so the aircraft was renumbered ZA947.

The Dakota continued in service with the RAE, and later the Defence Research Agency, until March 1992, when its future was placed under review. Significantly, it was the Colonel Commandant of The Parachute Regiment who wrote to the Chief of the Air Staff in October 1992 proposing that the disposal of the aircraft be delayed until after the 50th anniversary commemorations of the Normandy, Arnhem and VE-Day operations that were due to take place in 1994 and 1995. Meanwhile it could act as a training vehicle for Lancaster pilots as well as a useful utility transport for the Flight. A decision was made in March 1993 to add the aircraft to the BBMF for a two-year period, after which its future would be reviewed. Crewed by a pilot, a navigator and, when necessary, an air loadmaster, the Dakota is not displayed as such at air shows but it is employed for commemorative flypasts and parachute drops.

The Flight's Devon, VP981, first entered service in 1949 and is now the only one of its type remaining in RAF service. In 1985, following the disbandment of No 207 Squadron at RAF Northolt, it was allocated to the BBMF for communications duties and multi-engine continuation training and generally to assist in operations throughout the display season. However, the arrival of the Dakota has meant that the Devon will be grounded for a period so as to offset the costs of flying the larger aircraft.

The Flight's irreplaceable aircraft are maintained in display condition by a small number of dedicated engineers. Led by Warrant Officer Barry Sears, the team are all full-time members of the BBMF. WO Sears joined the Flight as the Engineering Officer in 1985 and is now in his thirty-eighth year with the RAF. Under his command is a Chief Technician (his deputy), one sergeant and nineteen tradesmen of the rank of Corporal or below. These latter comprise eight airframe fitters, eight engine fitters, two electricians and one communications tradesman. All

the engineers are volunteers and most are able to serve with the Flight for several years. The engine fitters have to undergo specialist training – a short course at Kidlington on piston engines and propellers – but the remaining tradesmen are left to develop their skills with experience.

The aircraft of the BBMF are maintained to an extremely high standard. All the lengthy maintenance schedules are carried out during the winter months, ensuring that the aircraft are available for the display season. Every six years each aircraft undergoes a 'Major' service, which is carried out under contract, away from Coningsby. This is the longest and most detailed of the servicing schedules which an aircraft has routinely to undergo. Each aircraft also has a 'Minor Star' service every two or three years, and this is completed at Coningsby. Both the Majors and the Minor Stars are

Right: Corporal Pete Jeffery is currently the longest-serving tradesman in the Flight. He is seen here (left) working inside PA474. (Alex Dickson)

Left: The sad result of LF363's crash-landing at Wittering in September 1991. Fortunately, the pilot escaped serious injury. (RAF Wittering)

lengthy affairs. The problems encountered will depend much on the number of hours an aircraft has flown since the last service, and of course the fact remains that as each service becomes due the aircraft's components will have aged and, perhaps, become more worn.

At the end of every display season the aircraft each undergo a 'Minor' servicing, consisting of a detailed inspection, and even during the season itself there are further inspections and routine servicing. After approximately every 50 flying hours each aircraft will receive a 'Primary Star' service and after every 25 hours a 'Primary'; both involve one or two days' work, carried out at a convenient time. All this attention represents maintenance of a very high standard.

Corporal Pete Jeffery, an airframe fitter, is the longest-serving tradesman

currently working with the Flight, having first joined it at Coltishall in 1974. He was posted to Shawbury in 1976 to work on Whirlwind and Gazelle helicopters but volunteered to return to the Flight in 1983: 'I have always enjoyed my time working on the Flight. To maintain historic aircraft is very interesting, particularly as an airframe fitter. Although some of the systems and flying controls are now obsolete, no specialist training is required and it is a matter of gaining more experience with time.'

During the winter months the engineers generally work daytime hours, Mondays to Fridays. However, during the display season each tradesman can expect to work long hours, to meet the flying display programme. There is also time spent away from his family, particularly when the Flight is displaying at weekends. 'We keep one crew available at Coningsby at all times,' explains Jeffery. 'This is known as the Base Crew and consists of one person from each trade – airframe, engines and electrician. The job of the Base Crew is to prepare the aircraft and to see them off. For the rest of the weekend the Crew provides trade coverage if required. When the Flight detaches away from Coningsby for displays, then we send tradesmen to look after the aircraft and to carry out any maintenance if required. On average, I expect to spend two or three short detachments away with the Flight each month during the display season.'

Fortunately, and perhaps surprisingly, there tend to be few problems maintaining the aircraft in terms of spares: 'Some components have to be made at the

Left: The Lancaster over Derwent Water in 1993 as part of the 50th anniversary commemoration of the Dams Raid. (Ian Frimston)

manufacturers,' says Jeffery, 'either from original drawings or, if these are not available . . . from the original piece. Our other source of spares is the general public, who very kindly donate parts to the Flight. Often these parts have been found lying around in lofts or garages . . . !'

All the display aircraft have limits placed on them in respect of the number of hours they may fly, to ensure that each may continue to perform for as many years as possible. The Spitfires are limited to a total of 180 hours spread among all five, each individual putting in no more than 60 hours. The Hurricane is also limited to 60 hours a season and the Lancaster to 85. All this means that time spent travelling to and from air displays has to be taken into consideration. When possible, therefore, the aircraft fly directly

to a venue. For the same reason, the Flight will try to co-ordinate things so that more than one display may be given in a day, to ensure that the maximum benefit is drawn from a given number of flying hours.

'Bids' from air show organizers for the BBMF to display are sent in writing to a Participation Committee in London. It is the task of the Committee to gather together all the bids for the following season and decide which events will be attended by which display teams. The Committee meets in January and forwards the proposed programme to the Flight, and it is then up to the Flight's staff and aircrew to make the final plans. Of course, the plans may, and probably will, change several times during the course of a season, but each year the BBMF

Below: The aircraft of the BBMF are maintained to an extremely high standard by a small number of voluntary engineers. (RAF Benson)

expects to attend some 200–300 events between May and September.

Co-ordinating all the displays and dealing with the daily enquiries to the BBMF office is a full-time task, particularly just before and during the display season. Looking after the administration of the Flight is Ted Farrant, a retired Air Electronics Officer with 34 years of RAF service, who is assisted by Yvonne Walker, a civil servant.

Because of increasing public interest and a demand for 'official tours' of the BBMF, tour guides were established in 1986, and by the following year a Visitors' Centre had been established to meet the public demand for facilities and merchandise connected with the Flight. One of the first people to become involved with this venture was Graham Wallen, a retired

RAF Flight Engineer with 26 years' service. He is now the manager of the Centre, employed full time by Lincolnshire County Council.

'The Visitors' Centre has proved a great success,' says Wallen. 'Each year we receive some 20,000 members of the public of all ages and from all backgrounds. Many visitors are ex-RAF from different parts of the world, some of whom have wartime experience on the aircraft types now on display. Equally, many of our visitors, young and old, have no connection with the RAF but simply want to see the aircraft close-up and to find out more about them. Financially the Centre is self-sustaining, and at the end of last year we were able to present profits of £3,000 to the RAF Benevolent Fund.'

During the peak season, July and August, the Centre is visited by as many as 300 people a day. The number of tour guides has increased to forty, plus reserves, most of whom are local ex-RAF personnel. Each guide spends one day a week at the Flight. The Centre is open from Monday to Friday, except on public holidays, and tours commence every hour, or every half-hour during the peak season, from 10 a.m. to 3 p.m. There is a small charge for a visit to the hangar, with concessionary rates for senior citizens and children, and there are facilities for the disabled. However, it is important to emphasize that there is no guarantee that a particular aircraft will be in the hangar on a specific day.

As with any RAF display team, the future of the BBMF is reviewed every four years. Obviously, it costs money to run the Flight – about £1–2 million a year

Fly Past, Fly Present

– and it could be considered by some to be an expensive luxury. Thus, in today's climate, the future of the Flight is never assured. However, the BBMF has brought, and will continue to bring, much pleasure to the thousands who see it every year. Whether they are inspected by former aircrew or watched in wonder by young enthusiasts at air shows, its aircraft remain a living memorial to the many thousands of airmen who gave their lives in the service of their country . . . 'lest we forget'.

The Last Flying B-23

The slippery lines of the Douglas B-23 Dragon epitomize late 1930s Army Air Corps aviation. Man had taken to the skies only thirty-six years before the B-23 made its first flight on 27 July 1939. Thirty-eight Dragons were constructed at Douglas's Santa Monica, California, assembly line, with Air Corps serial numbers 39-27 to 39-64 inclusive, the last being delivered from Clover Field to the Army Air Corps in September 1940.

The Dragon was a twin-engine medium bomber developed from the 1935 Douglas B-18 design. The B-18 is best described as 'portly', having a wing span of 89 feet 6 inches and a fuselage length of 56 feet 8 inches. Powered by a pair of 810-horsepower Wright R-1820-45 radials, the aircraft had a top speed of 217mph at 10,000 feet. Had there been a war at the time, the slow, lumbering B-18 would have had to face Germany's new Messerschmitt Bf 109B-2. The latter would see service in the Spanish Civil War beginning in the summer of 1937 and was capable of 289mph at 13,120 feet – more than a match for the

B-18. The Army needed a faster bomber, based on fighter performance, and Douglas proposed a B-18A with R-2600-1 engines which would have been designated B-22. However, the B-22 was dropped in favour of the B-23, the funding for which came from the cancelled project (which was part of the B-18 contract).

Although wings and horizontal surfaces similar to the B-18's were used in the B-23, the Dragon was a completely new aeroplane. The fuselage was reduced in width and streamlined, a new vertical fin and rudder was incorporated and fully retractable landing gear was installed in the nacelles under each supercharged 1,600-horsepower Wright R-2600-3 radial engine. The R-2600-3s pulled the Dragon

Above: N747M at an unidentified location in the early 1960s. (Ed Davies)

aircraft to be obsolete: the new four-engine Boeing B-17s and Consolidated B-24s were already working their way on to the inventory by the end of 1940.

The 17th Bomb Group, head-quartered at March Field, was the first AAC unit to receive the Douglas B-23 Dragon. The Group's squadrons – the 34th, 37th and 95th Bomb Squadrons – flew the B-23 from March Field in California, McChord Field in Washington and Pendleton in Oregon. When the 17th Bomb Group re-equipped with North American B-25 Mitchells in the summer of 1940, the B-23s were passed to the 12th Bomb Group at McChord Field in January 1941. After the Japanese attack on Pearl Harbor on 7 December 1941, the Dragons flew anti-submarine warfare patrols off the west coast. They were considered by Doolittle for the Tokyo raid, but the aircraft's wing span was too great to clear the island on the USS Hornet's deck so the B-25 was chosen instead. The B-23s were subsequently transferred to the 13th Bomb Group at Orlando, Florida, and flew anti-submarine warfare and coastal convoy escort duties for the remainder of the war. However, throughout its wartime patrols the B-23 never saw combat.

The Dragon also served in the transport role, Army brass appreciating the speed of the aircraft and converting seventeen (serial numbers 39-29, -31, -34, -35, -38, -39, -41, -43, -47, -54, -55, -56, -57, -58, -59, -63 and -64) to UC-67 configuration. UC-67s had their armour plate and machine guns removed, and an interior was fitted to accommodate passengers and cargo. After the war ended in September 1945, a number of American corporations ex-

through the sky at a top speed of 282mph at 12,000 feet – 65mph faster than the B-18. The B-23 had a service ceiling of 31,000 feet, and the offensive armament consisted of three .30-calibre machine guns, at nose, dorsal and ventral hatches, plus a single .50-calibre machine gun in the tail – the first time such a position had been incorporated in an Army Air Corps bomber. In the B-23 the tail gunner reclined, his feet facing aft, and he sighted down the barrel of the gun. Side panels opened like a vertical clam shell into the slipstream to increase his field of vision. Carrying a 4,000lb bomb load, the B-23 was reportedly capable of a range of 1,400 miles. Before the last B-23 was delivered, however, the Air Corps considered the

pressed interest in the B-23 as a high-speed executive transport, and the Civil Aviation Authority issued Memo 2-576 on 28 November 1945 approving the B-23 for civilian operations. Sixteen B-23s and four UC-78s quickly appeared on the civil register; General Electric was the largest operator, with a fleet of two B-23s (N33310 and N33311) and a UC-67 (N45361). Howard Hughes converted a number of the aircraft to executive configuration. The conversion included state-of-the-art avionics, a dual-control cockpit (the Army flew with a single pilot plus a flight engineer), seating for eight to twelve passengers, a four-seat folding table, a mini-galley or wet bar, a three-seat divan and a lavatory – luxurious aviation accommodation by any standards. B-23s served as executive transports until the mid-1960s when the Learjet became an alternative source of corporate transportation.

The seventh Douglas B-23 to roll off the company's Santa Monica assembly line was Army Air Forces serial number 39-33. Delivered to the Army on 28 May

Left: B-23 N747M wears a non-standard radar nose installed in the late 1940s when the aircraft was converted from a bomber to an executive transport. (Nicholas Veronico)
Right: N747M in flight over the central Californian foothills. The B-23's skin is polished to a highly reflective finish. This aircraft is the only pre-Second World War US bomber flying. (Nicholas Veronico)

1940, the Dragon was assigned to Aberdeen Proving Ground, Maryland, where it participated in munitions testing, including trial drops of the 2,000lb blockbuster bombs. The Army Air Forces earmarked 39-33 as surplus and flew the plane to the Reclamation Finance Corporation's sales yard at McKellar Field, Jackson, Tennessee, on 2 December 1944. When it landed it had accumulated only 1,140 hours of flight time.

Howard Hughes' late 1940s and 1950s aircraft fleet included a couple of B-23s,

39-33 one of them. Hughes had purchased 39-33 from the Reclamation Finance Corporation for $20,000, and on 2 June 1945 the aircraft was registered as NC49548. Hughes quickly turned it around and sold it to Gar Wood Industries of Detroit, Michigan, who then contracted with Hughes to convert the aircraft to executive configuration, which included the removal of all military equipment and the addition of co-pilot's controls – a stipulation of the Civil Aviation Authority (now Federal Aviation Administration) to allow

Left: The front office of the B-23. The screen in the centre is the Collins colour radar. (Nicholas Veronico)

Below: Basic flight instruments in the rear cabin gave passengers the answers to their most common questions – 'How high are we?' and 'How fast are we going?' (Nicholas Veronico)

the aircraft to operate in the 'standard' airworthiness category as an executive transport – a Collins 101 radar in the nose and updated R-2600-29 radial engines. Less than three years later, on 19 February 1948, 39-33 was sold to Lehman Brothers of New York for $5,000 and re-registered NC747; Lehmans re-sold the Dragon to Hughes, for $25,000, on 6 September 1948.

After this quick succession of owners, 39-33 was purchased by the Food Machinery & Chemical Corporation (the later FMC Corporation) of McAllen, Texas. FMC flew the B-23 all over the United States as one of their primary transports for corporate executives. After fourteen years of faithful service, FMC donated the B-23 to The Oxford Group/ Moral Rearmament Inc of New York City on 26 January 1965; at the same time the aircraft was re-registered N747M. Monarch Aviation, of Monterey, California, purchased it on 19 February 1966 and ten months later re-sold it to Thomas H. Hudson, who operated the plane from Monterey under the company name 'Douglas B-23 of Monterey' for twelve years until he passed away. It was then sold to World Airways on 1 May 1978.

World Airways used the B-23 as an executive transport for the airline's founder, Ed Daly, and as a nostalgic marketing tool. Crews took the B-23 to every air show possible, allowing the public to tour the aircraft in exchange for a brochure on the airline. In 1976 World Airways spent $200,000 overhauling N747M. The interior configuration and radio/ avionics package was retained, as was the Hughes cockpit configuration. Most of the work involved corrosion control. Mike Bogue, president of Power Pac Engineering, of Ione, California, acquired the B-23 in 1987 after the death of World Airways' President, Daly. Today, Bogue flies the B-23 to as many air shows as possible in an effort to bring this historic, one-of-a-kind bomber to the public. Although Bogue is a rated pilot and has about 200 hours in the B-23, he has recently turned over pilot-in-command duties to Denny Ghiringhelli, an American Airlines captain.

Pilot/owner Bogue and a team of volunteers maintain the aircraft. The B-23's crew chief is Wayne Cook, who is assisted by Bob Whalen, responsible for maintaining the machine's polished exterior; Ted Curiel, who maintains the engines, landing gear and other major systems; and Jacqi Ng, who has been assisting with the tail turret restoration.

'Money and work – that's what it takes to keep the B-23 in the air,' says Cook. 'The biggest problem in running an airplane this old is parts. The exhaust system on the B-23 is a prime example. It's similar to the DC-4's, where the collector is bolted rigidly to the airplane, and yet you have to allow for minor movements of the engine. To allow the engine flexibil-ity, Douglas engineers used a double ball-socket arrangement – where you have a straight pipe between the collector and the engine with a ball joint at either end. Since only thirty-eight B-23s were built, and the exhaust was built exclusively for this airframe, parts are in short supply. We are to the point now where we are kicking around the idea of changing the exhaust system due to the lack of replacement parts. We'll have to do something fairly soon – I think within the next two or three years. As the exhaust ball joints get carboned-up they freeze, and then the joint breaks and they won't pivot any more. Either we are going to have to custom-make some replacements, or replace the exhaust system with something else.'

Above: Owner Mike Bogue and Denny Ghiringhelli at the controls of the preserved Douglas B-23. The aircraft was operated by Howard Hughes and also by Edward Daly, the late President of World Airways. (Nicholas Veronico)

Douglas B-23 Dragon Survivors

Model	Serial	Reg	Owner	Status
B-23	39-051	N534J	Pima Air Museum, Tucson, Az	Public view
B-23	39-036	N52327	McChord AFB Museum, Tacoma, Wa	Public view
B-23	39-045	N880L	Castle AFB Museum, Atwater, Ca	Public view
B-23	39-057	N4000B	Weeks Air Museum, Miami, Fla	In storage
B-23	39-037	N800N	USAF Museum, Dayton, Oh	Public view
UC-67	39-038	N62G	CAF, Midland, Texas	In storage
B-23	39-033	N747M	Mike Bogue, Ione, Ca	Airworthy
B-23	39-046	N53253	Robert Schafeli, Moses Lake, Wa	In storage

Bogue and Cook are considering modifying a TBM Avenger exhaust system to fit. The modification would require two TBM exhausts for each B-23 engine – an expensive and time-consuming process, but Cook is the man for the job. He works as a metal fabricator at the Lawrence Livermore National Laboratory and previously worked in the sheet metal shops for United Airlines for thirteen years. Little parts such as the tail wheel locking pin are also of concern. Probably a $2 part in the 1930s, it will cost hundreds to have a new one machined. 'Each year we have to do an annual, which entails pulling every inspection plate and panel off the airplane,' explains Cook. 'With the airplane open we look inside for any corrosion, damage, cracks, loose fasteners, anything like that. We crawl inside the airplane, pulling as much of the belly open as we can. This allows us to inspect all of the control cables (checking for frayed cables), lube the pulleys and all of the bearings in the control surfaces, perform a compression check on the engines and inspect the exhaust system, looking for heat damage or cracks. We

are always looking for corrosion. That's the biggest thing right now.'

Bogue reports that when Douglas constructed the B-23 they used a lot of dissimilar metals, for example stainless steel against aluminium. Although this makes for a very rugged aircraft, it causes inner granular corrosion. The B-23 was also stored at Northern California's Oakland Airport, right on the San Francisco Bay, and the salt air environment quickly promoted corrosion. The major problem has been in the engine nacelles, and that has been because of the dissimilar metals. 'I've replaced one longeron in the right-hand nacelle and I've got one in the left-hand to do,' says Cook. 'They have aluminum and stainless steel next to each other – at the time the plane was built they did not put a coat of primer in between.'

Always on the look-out for B-23 parts, Cook relates a story about a possible treasure trove of B-23 parts. 'This gentleman came up to the plane and introduced himself at the Portland Rose Festival air show (Oregon) in 1990. He said that he was a radio operator during World War II and he made only one flight in a B-23. His squadron, the 17th Bomb Group, normally flew B-25s. They needed a radio operator on this particular training flight, so he went along. They got lost in a blizzard and ended up bellying the B-23 in on a frozen lake. After setting down on frozen Loon Lake (Idaho), the B-23 slid up into the tree line, shearing the outer wings off. The radio operator and one other guy hiked out. It was nine days before they got rescued and everybody survived.'

Cook and Bogue knew about the B-23 crash and have studied detailed photos of the site. They are planning an expedition there to obtain parts which will aid the restoration. Many components can be used straight from the wreck while others will serve as templates for new ones. 'The airplane has been up there all this time,' reveals Cook. 'The only way you can get to the crash site is on horseback or hike. We would like to retrieve as many parts as possible, including parts and fittings from the tail turret, any exhaust ball joints, and the tail wheel assembly.'

The B-23's excellent condition will allow it to be flown for quite a while. Cook is slowly restoring the tail turret as the required components are located. He explains that the aircraft is '. . . a flying restoration. We try to keep the airplane in the air and make progress on the restoration at the same time. At this time we do not have any plans to reconvert the plane to the stock bombardier's nose configuration.'

The only enemies the B-23 has are the cost of fuel and spare parts. Bogue welcomes the skills and talents of anyone willing to volunteer his time to the B-23

project. 'At economical cruise we burn 135 gallons per hour and, unfortunately, we can't afford to fly it for fun,' explains Cook. 'We usually just take it out when we are going to an air show where we are getting gas. It is difficult to try to fly it [due to the gas factor].'

The one location you can count on seeing the B-23 is on the ramp at the National Championship Air Races held each September in Reno, Nevada. Cruising at 220mph and with an oxygen system for all passengers, Bogue flies the B-23 as

Below: Plush executive seating in the forward passenger compartment of the B-23. (Nicholas Veronico)

Below: The B-23 was the first US Army Air Corps bomber to feature a tail turret, which boasted a single .50-calibre machine gun. Crew Chief Wayne Cook is slowly restoring this position. (Nicholas Veronico)

the support ship for Tom Camp's Yak-11 racer Maniyak. Reno is just a short hop over the Sierra Nevada mountains to Reno, from Bogue's California home. The B-23 can haul the crew, their gear and spare parts with ease. With the warbird exterior and executive interior, the crew travels in style.

Mike Bogue's B-23 is the only example of a pre-war US Army Air Corps bomber flying today and will probably be the only flying Dragon for some time to come.

Douglas B-23

Wing span: 92ft (28.04m)
Length: 58ft 4in (17.78m)
Height: 18ft 6in (5.64m)
Wing area: 993 sq ft (92.2m²)
Weights: Maximum 30,475lb (13,820kg)
Speed: Maximum 282mph (454kph), cruising 210mph (338kph)
Range: 1,445 miles (2,326km)
Powerplant: Two 1,700hp Wright Cyclone 14-cylinder R-2600-29 radials

---

Classic Warbirds

Philip Handleman

Below: *A grand military design from the Golden Age of Flight is the F3F-2, the last of Grumman's biplane fighters. One of three such aircraft painstakingly rebuilt by Herb Tischler's Texas Airplane Factory in Fort Worth, this example belongs to the Lone Star Flight Museum. Powered by a 1,000-* *horsepower Wright R-1820, the Grumman is a fast climber and can cruise at 200mph, but pilots warn that the aircraft is unforgiving on the ground because of the lack of forward visibility, the close-coupled landing gear and the incredible torque. (Philip Handleman)*

Above and below: *The N3N is similar in appearance to a Stearman, for which it is often mistaken. However, the N3N, manufactured by the Naval Aircraft Factory in Philadelphia, has four ailerons, two on each wing, and aileron connecting struts immediately aft of the 'N' struts. The standard Navy training colour during the Second World War was yellow, and two-seat, open-cockpit biplane trainers, whether Stearmans or N3Ns, were nicknamed 'Yellow Peril'. Green striping identified those aircraft which were equipped with instruments. (Philip Handleman)*

Left: One of the world's largest gatherings of biplanes takes place every year in early September at the small west central Illinois town of Galesburg – the National Stearman Fly-In. Up to 120 of the famous Second World War Stearman trainers have attended the event and, lined up row upon row on the grass field, the brightly coloured aircraft are a sight to behold. (Philip Handleman)

Below: Sounding like a flying washing machine when airborne, the North American T-28 was the last of the radial-engine trainers in service with the US military. This gleaming example participated at Oshkosh 1992. (Philip Handleman)

Classic Warbirds

Left: *The sights and sounds familiar to flying cadets and instructor pilots of the Second World War can now be recreated only at air shows. The rumble of a squadron's radial-engine trainers was common at places like Kelly Field and Randolph Field in the early 1940s, when global conflict required the services of tens of thousands of qualified flight personnel. These days, formation teams like the* Six of Diamonds, *flying the AT-6, bring those spine-tingling moments back to life. The step-echelon formation pictured here was part of the team's performance at Oshkosh in 1989. (Philip Handleman)*

Below: *Quaint for a warbird, the Cessna Bobcat of the Second World War was employed as a multi-engine trainer for students moving up to bombers and transports. Because of its wooden construction it was also known as the 'Bamboo Bomber'. This shining example was seen in the warbird parade at Oshkosh in 1993. (Philip Handleman)*

Left, upper: *Among the primary trainers employed by the US military during the Second World War was the Fairchild PT-19, the enclosed-cockpit version of which was designated PT-26. This PT-26 was seen at Geneseo Airport in New York during the 1990 warbird show. The site's 5,000-foot long grass strip was ideal for the participants and the event had a home-town 'folksiness', but unfortunately a dispute involving nearby property forced the organizers to switch the 1994 show to Batavia. (Philip Handleman)*

Left, lower: *A regular visitor at Oshkosh has been the* grande dame *of warbird pilots, the Kalamazoo Aviation History Museum's Sue Parish. Her distinctive pink P-40 is unmistakable. Allegedly, the colour scheme originated in the fact that the paintwork covering P-40s stationed in North Africa during the war turned a shade of pink after exposure to the oppressive sun. Sue Parish pursued*

flying from an early age and flew for the Army during the war. She has performed her graceful aerobatic routine in front of millions of spectators over the years, and this appearance at Oshkosh in 1993 was one of her last before she retired from active participation at air shows. (Philip Handleman)

Above: *The North American AT-6 Texan was otherwise known as the 'pilot maker'. As US cadets progressed from primary, through basic to advanced training they would get the opportunity to fly this aircraft, introducing them to higher speeds and more complex systems. This AT-6 was seen at Oshkosh in 1992, its polished aluminium skin and countless rivets glistening in the afternoon Wisconsin sun. Note the 'Hat-in-the-Ring' insignia on the fuselage, borrowed from Eddie Rickenbacker's legendary 94th Aero Squadron. (Philip Handleman)*

Left, upper: *Its sleek, twin-boom configuration has always made the P-38 Lightning stand out, but there are only about half a dozen still flying. Long-time show and racing pilot Lefty Gardner flies an all-white P-38 that he calls* White Lit'nin, *and this beautiful aeroplane is often seen at the Reno air races and at CAF events. (Philip Handleman)*

Left, lower: *A magnificent Avenger, a licence-built TBM, ploughs through the humid skies over Harlingen in 1989. One of the US Navy's premier torpedo bombers of the Second World War, this sturdy aircraft originated in the Grumman Iron-works and was highly regarded for its ability to absorb damage from enemy fire. Perhaps the most famous Avenger pilot is former US President George Bush. (Philip Handleman)*

Right, upper: *A popular air show performance is the re-enactment of the Japanese attack on Pearl Harbor in a routine called 'Tora! Tora! Tora!' This replica 'Kate' torpedo bomber is one of many aircraft that perform in concert with rip-roaring pyrotechnics to present a realistic portrayal of aerial combat. The jungle camouflage on this aircraft's fuselage made for a uniquely colourful sight at the 1990 Wings of Eagles show at Geneseo, New York. (Philip Handleman)*

Right: The B-25, an Army Air Forces medium bomber, was chosen for the first aerial raid on Japan because it had a greater bomb-load than any carrier-based Navy aircraft at the time. The twin-engine bomber was, in a historical irony, named after Billy Mitchell, the controversial Army officer who many years earlier had forecast a Sunday attack on US forces at Pearl Harbor. Today B-25s are a common sight at the big warbird air shows; this one made numerous low passes at the 1989 Chino event. (Philip Handleman)

Above: *In 1992 the organizers of the Oshkosh air show decided to honour Jimmy Doolittle's Tokyo Raiders since this was the 50th anniversary of their daring attack. The aged raiders were invited to attend, and nine B-25s re-enacted the fateful mission. As part of the ceremony, this Mitchell simulated the take-off from the heaving deck of the USS Hornet. (Philip Handleman)*

Below: *Waves of P-51s take to the sky as part of the warbird displays during the week at Oshkosh. These aircraft, arguably the best all-round piston-engine fighters of the Second World War, were the favourite mount of many Allied pilots. Equipped with external fuel tanks, they escorted bombers far into enemy territory, helping to assure the safety of those vital missions. (Philip Handleman)*

Above: *The Hawker Sea Fury was one of the fastest piston-engine production aircraft, and, not surprisingly, several compete each year in the Unlimited Class at Reno. The Sea Fury here, called* Cottonmouth, *is enjoying a respite with its wings folded. (Philip Handleman)*

Left: *An attention-getter at Oshkosh in 1992 was Vern Raburn's Lockheed C-121A Constellation. Based at Scottsdale, Arizona, this massive four-engine cargo plane has been restored in the colours of the US Military Air Transport Service (MATS). This 'Connie' is one of only two flying now. As a fund-raising venture, flying lessons are offered in this aircraft: ground school and one hour of flight time start at $3,995. (Philip Handleman)*

Left, lower: *Jets are increasingly common at warbirds air shows. The classic lines of the North American F-86 are apparent in this picture of a Canadian-built Sabre restored as an F-86E in the colours of famed US ace Frederick C. 'Boots' Blesse. General Blesse scored ten victories during the Korean War and wrote a widely read tactics primer that hammered home the truism 'No guts, no glory'. In 1992 the aircraft's then owner, John Dilley, and his restoration crew received the Reserve Grand Champion Warbird award. (Philip Handleman)*

Below: *The EAA warbird collection is brimming with priceless artefacts. The Eagle Hangar, which is an addition to the organization's Air Adventure Museum, houses the core of the rich Second World War-period collection. This Piasecki 'Flying Banana', one of the many gems on static display, stands guard near the hangar's entrance. (Philip Handleman)*

Flying the Past

Nicholas Veronico/Colin Dodds

The National Air and Space Museum in Washington, DC, and the Champlin Fighter Museum in Mesa, Arizona, house the two largest collections of original First World War aircraft in the United States. These pristine machines are on display all year round. But where do you go to experience a living, breathing, flying World War I aero-plane? Air shows and your local airport may just be the ticket, thanks to people like Jim Nissen. Nissen owns and flies a Curtiss JN-4 Jenny from Meadowlark Airport, Livermore, California. Currently undergoing an extensive rebuild, this 'stringbag' (with a small 'S') will now be able to fly well into the twenty-first century . . .

Below: The Jenny in the collection of General William Lyons, based at Orange County Airport in southern California. (Nicholas Veronico)

When the US Army began to expand its aviation resources prior to its entry into World War I, Curtiss offered the JN, a combination of the better features of its J and N models. The Army purchased a small number of JNs in 1914 for the observation role. The N model would continue to be produced throughout the war years, but the JNs would dominate Curtiss production and a total of 6,070 Jennys were built during the war years. Today, about 35 survive, with as many as seven maintained in flyable condition.

The Jenny flew with the US Army until September 1927, when the type was eliminated from the inventory. After the war, hundreds of surplus Jennys were bought up by ex-military flyers and used to barnstorm across the United States. The silent movies of the early 1920s are filled with the antics of these daredevils as car-to-plane transfers via a rope ladder suspended beneath a Jenny and plane-to-plane transfers by wing-walkers graced the silver screen. This barnstorming age, from 1920 to 1926, is known as 'The Jenny Era'. 'You don't fly it, you drive it,' says Nissen. 'It flies like a truck. You have to be ahead of this airplane, not because it's going fast, but because it reacts slow.'

Nissen's Jenny, serial number 5002, was part of a 1917 order for 400 JN-4Ds which were produced by the Springfield Aircraft Company of Springfield, Missouri. Springfield were the largest builder of JN-4s, behind Curtiss and its Canadian subsidiary the Curtiss Aeroplane & Motor Company, having built 485 JN-4Ds during the war years. Each Jenny on this order cost $4,954.34. Number 5002 was the twenty-seventh Jenny built by Springfield. In the late 1950s Nissen acquired a number of ex-First World War aircraft, including the Jenny and a Thomas-Morse S4C, N5858. While restoring and flying the Thomas-Morse (or 'Tommy', as the little biplane fighters are popularly called), Nissen stored the Jenny. He flew the 'Tommy' for a number of years and eventually a buyer offered 'the right amount' and the aeroplane was sold. The 'Tommy' was eventually traded to the Naval Aviation Museum at Pensacola, Florida, where she can be seen today on display – a fact Nissen is not to happy with as he would like to have seen the nimble fighter remain airworthy, flying in her natural element.

Referring to the rarity of flying First World War-era aircraft, Nissen says that the only way to acquire one is through either a death or a divorce: he believes that anyone who flies one will never part with it. After the 'Tommy' left his stable of aircraft, he began the task of restoring 5002. He obtained original components, and when he had finished, ninety per cent of the aircraft was made from original parts. The only modification Nissen made – and this is not visible even to the trained eye – is the 'steerable' tail skid. The mechanism for this is housed inside the fuselage, and its presence is only apparent if close attention is paid to the aircraft on landing.

The restored Jenny made its debut in 1976, and Nissen has dedicated his retire-ment to bringing his First World War trainer to the public. Nissen is the only Jenny pilot/owner who performs any aerobatics at air shows. His routine includes loops, wing-overs and spins. He usually does about ten or twelve spin turns from about 2,000 feet. The Jenny just floats like a leaf on the way down. Nissen had considered flying his Jenny back to Oshkosh, but after methodically planning the trip he reluctantly gave up the idea. When he broached his dream of making this trip, a friend suggested that he first fly a Stearman back to the Experimental Aircraft Association's annual Fly-In to map out the route, but during his Stearman trip to Oshkosh Nissen realized that there were very few grass strips for the Jenny to land on; this, plus the height of the mountains and the type of terrain he would have to fly over, killed the idea. Nissen did fly the Jenny to 11,000 feet in an attempt to see if he could clear the mountains between California and Colorado. Considering that the Jenny is rated for a service ceiling of 6,500 feet, 11,000 feet is most impressive.

When not tinkering with or showing the Jenny to the public, Nissen takes great pride in sharing his knowledge with others interested in the early era of aviation: for him, passing on the traditions and skills of flying the Jenny is part of the fun of owning such an aircraft. Nissen's daughter Sallie and son-in-law Zach Taylor are his most willing students. The latter says of his father-in law, 'In the 500 hours or so Jim has flown the airplane, he has given 1,000 to 1,500 rides. That's what pleases him as much as anything else – to see a passenger climb out of the cockpit,

Right: Jim Nissen enjoys flying the Jenny, only seven of which are thought to be airworthy today. In this series of photographs, note that a tail wheel has been fitted to the skid for operations from a concrete runway. (Nicholas Veronico)

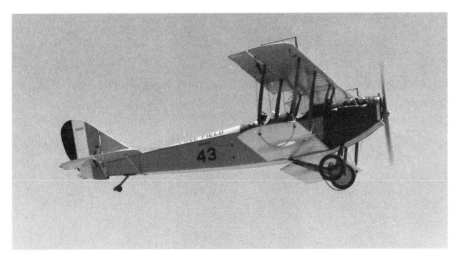

see the smile on his face, and have him shake his hand, saying, "That's the greatest airplane ride I've had in my entire life!" I started flying the Jenny eight, maybe nine years ago and I may have between 125 and 140 hours in it. By today's standards I've got quite a bit of [Jenny] time. There's no communication in the Jenny, so when Jim and I were flying dual together somehow he always made it known just exactly what he wanted me to do – and what I wasn't doing right.' Nissen would communicate by pointing, shaking the stick, and pounding on the rudder bar to get Taylor, and others who were getting checked out, to perform properly.

'I really do enjoy flying the Jenny,' continues Taylor. 'It is just a wonderful airplane, a totally different experience than any other in aviation. I've only been flying about fourteen or fifteen years, in maybe twenty different types of small, single-engine aircraft, but as far as I'm concerned it is the consummate airplane to fly. The Jenny teaches you what airplanes are really about, how to fly them, how to stay out of trouble, and what happens if you don't fly them properly. The Jenny is an airplane where you use every bit of your senses to tell what's going on. Obviously, with no airspeed indicator or artificial horizon, you've just got to depend on visual references, the seat of your pants, the straw coming off the floor – all kinds of things tell you what attitude you're in.

'It's actually a pretty gentle airplane to fly. It reacts slowly to anything you do, so you do need to stay ahead of it, planning where you want the airplane to go.

On the other hand, it is an airplane that's totally unstable. If you take your hands and feet off the controls of most small airplanes, basically the wings will level themselves, the nose will come up, and the plane will seek an attitude it wants. In the Jenny, if you take your feet and hands off of the controls, it might bank to the right, it might bank to the left, the nose might come up, it might go down. So you constantly fly it by attitude and visual reference. You push on the stick or pull on it, add in aileron or take it out to keep it in the attitude you want.'

The Jenny's landing roll depends on the surface – its hardness or softness. In winter, using the grass strip at Nissen's Livermore Airport, the Jenny will very easily stop in 600 feet. In the summer and autumn, when the ground has been baked hard, sometimes it takes a little more than 900 feet, which puts the landing roll right up on the asphalt apron. 'One of the things we train doing when Jim is teaching us to fly the airplane is an intentional ground loop as the airplane slows down,' says Taylor. 'It just brings you around, slows you down, and you stop. It works very nicely.'

How the ground loop affects the landing gear structure depends on how the manoeuvre is executed: 'It all depends on

Left and right: The Jenny nears completion of its 1993–94 overhaul. The fuselage is finished and awaits the installation of a new cowling. (Nicholas Veronico)

Left: The rear cockpit, state-of-the-art for its time. (Nicholas Veronico)

Above: Detail of the Jenny's radiator and propeller hub. (Nicholas Veronico)

attended flight school at Naval Air Station Pensacola, Florida, before joining the Fleet. He flew briefly with Pan Am World Airways on the trans-Pacific routes and he joined NACA (National Advisory Committee for Aeronautics) as a test pilot and aeronautical engineer prior to American involvement in the Second World War. During his tenure at NACA, Nissen flew every type of US military aircraft built during the war. His expertise in maintaining the engine and rebuilding the aircraft's structure have been used to supervise others new to the process of restoring a First World War-era biplane.

The Jenny's rebuild should be completed soon and the biplane will be back in the air by the time these words are published. Prior to the 1993–94 rebuild, ninety per cent of the wood in the aircraft was over seventy years old. It was suffering from fatigue, and it was also time to re-cover the structure. Today, fifty per cent of the wood is new and the Jenny is probably in better condition than when it was restored with all original pieces in the early 1970s. 'We are pretty proud of the workmanship on the whole airplane – everybody has done a wonderful job,' enthuses Taylor.

The aircraft is built upside-down – the top longeron is straight and the bottom longeron has a curve in it. Thus the airframe is attached to the jig with the top longeron down, the rest of the fuselage being built from the fuselage stations down. 'The hardest thing to rebuilding the Jenny was keeping track of things as they came apart,' recalls Taylor. 'There are twelve stations on the airplane and at

how you do it, the speed you do it at, and how quickly you bring the plane around. If it's done properly, the way its taught by Jim, it's not hard on the gear at all.' This is one of the many nuances to flying a First World War 'stringbag' that must be passed from pilot to pilot – one that cannot be taught by reading the technique from a book.

Nissen's vast experience plays a major role in teaching new pilots and mechanics how to fly and maintain the Jenny. He was a Navy aviator and who

each station there are at least four fittings and sometimes more – roughly fifty fittings in the fuselage. On each fitting there is at least one wire that comes off of it and one turnbuckle. You look at the complexity of the thing, labelling the pieces that come off, keeping track of them, then sandblasting, beadblasting and painting every part and bringing it back up to speed. The rebuilding process is quite amazing. Basically, once we got started – and we've had lots of help – it fell into place pretty easily.'

Maintaining the 90-horsepower Curtiss OX-5 engine is quite a feat. The engine is fairly simple in operation, being a water-cooled V-8 with an exposed rocker arm mechanism and a single magneto. Jim Nissen has maintained it since he put it together. His background as an aeronautical engineer gives him the skills and knowledge to do it. 'When I came along he taught me about engines, especially that particular engine,' says Taylor. 'He and I have done the top end on it a couple of times and I watched him do the lower end once. So I've been completely through the whole engine, but, once again, parts for an engine that's over seventy years old are obviously hard to come by. Over the years Jim has bought two or three spare engines, and we have a number of spare cylinders. So we could build a new OX-5 out of the parts we have if we needed to.'

Taylor sums up the Jenny experience by saying, 'It's something to see the old airplanes fly and keep 'em in the air. I have an appreciation for that. It's a real privilege for me to be able to fly the airplane. I feel very fortunate.'

Curtiss JN-4D Jenny 5002

Wing span: 43ft 7³/₈in (13.29m)
Length: 27ft 4in (8.33m)
Height: 9ft 10⁵/₈in (3.01m)
Wing area: 352 sq ft (32.7m²)
Weights: Empty 1,390lb (630.49kg), gross 1,920lb (870.89kg)
Speed: Maximum 75mph (120.69kph), cruising 60mph (96.55kph)
Service ceiling: 6,500ft (1,981m)

Left: Nissen adjusts a fuselage turnbuckle during the reassembly process. This restoration will ensure that the Jenny continues to fly into the next century. (Nicholas Veronico)

Right: The Jenny is flown solo from the rear seat. During training, the instructor sat in the front cockpit. Note the spartan instruments. (Nicholas Veronico)

Fly Past, Fly Present

Sixty Years On

Aviation has its fair share of characters, both human and mechanical. It is the mechanical ones, the aeroplanes, that are particularly fascinating, because of the surprisingly personal characteristics possessed by some individual aircraft within types. Usually the outstanding characters can be expected to come from the ranks of the charismatic fighter and bomber types, but one transport model in particular that seems to have been promoted from the lower ranks of interesting aircraft is the De Havilland DH 89 Dragon Rapide, first flown sixty years ago. In a promotional brochure, the makers blandly described their new 1934 Rapides as 'Light twin engine biplanes of wood and fabric construction, equipped with a cabin arranged for eight passengers and a pilot. They are powered with two Gipsy Queen III engines driving fixed-pitch propellers.'

This uninspiring description does not correspond with the strength of interest that would subsequently be shown by so many people in what might be presumed to be a relatively boring old biplane. There is, today, great interest in this wood and fabric transport, as exemplified by the surprising number of positive comments made about a recently restored Rapide. Over a period of a few weeks, seven people, at unrelated events, when hearing about the Rapide in question, came alive with excitement in telling their own stories of how they remembered the type with great affection. Most had taken their first flight in a Rapide at the early London Airport, or at Land's End; some had remembered the pioneering communica-

tions work done by the aircraft post-war; some had maintained it; and others had flown it. But not one of the memories recalled the noisy, cramped cabin, the slow and turbulent flights, the poor head-room or the rather alarming lack of performance. Without exception, all who remembered the aircraft expressed a great affection for the old girl, mentioning that it was quaint, old-fashioned and small but that it had surprisingly comfortable, leather-covered seats and that there was a unique intimacy, with the pilot sitting up front in his cockpit, within shouting distance of his passengers. Each was fascinated by its feeling of 'character'. Is this stirring of interest among those who have flown in Rapides reflected in the attitudes of those who operated it? A view from the aircraft's front seat may provide a feeling for the pilot's relationship with this bland old bird.

The appearance of this machine is like no other, if one discounts its larger, chubbier four-engine predecessor, the D.H.86 Express. The unique, 1930s lines and curves, as the aircraft stands ready for flight, reveal a paradoxical design. The smoothly flowing shapes of fuselage, engine cowlings moulded into undercarriage 'trousers' and elegantly tapered wings are examples of aerodynamic efficiency, designed to be drag-reducing, so permitting higher speeds. Yet this two-and-a-half-ton aircraft sprouts two pairs of 48-foot wings and a plethora of struts, double bracing wires, exposed fittings and other excrescences, all sitting out in the airflow and each adding to the already high, inefficient drag. They all add to the charm, but surely the extra aerodynamic

drag must have outweighed the practi-
calities of the well streamlined shapes?
Would the same engines and load capacity, combined with a neat cantilever
monoplane wing and total adherence to
streamlining, have produced better range,
a higher speed and a better single-engine
performance? It would appear that, in the
end, the advantages of retaining existing
manufacturing processes and materials,
and the operating experience already
gained with the Rapide's siblings, the
Dragon and the Express, made better
streamlining seem unnecessary in the
early 1930s: the design performed well
enough when tested, so refinement would
merely have added to the purchase price
in a very competitive market.

It was quite fortuitous that no further changes were made, as the whole
appearance of the aircraft is delightfully
De Havilland. Who else could have drawn
that complex combination of flat glass
panels and curved wooden structure
which forms the pilot's pulpit, or around

the engine cowls, which seem to melt into
the undercarriage struts and encompass
the fuel and oil tanks in passing. No other
designer could have produced the elegant
lines flowing rearwards from the wide
fuselage into the tall, DH-trademark fin
and rudder in such a stylish way. But
what about the view from inside?

Once the administrative and external preliminaries are tidied up, the pilot
reaches up to open the small cabin entrance door on the port side. The first
sensation is one of quality, aided by the
luxurious aroma of the leather seats and
the typical DH-style grey and green fur-
nishings, executed with subtle good taste
– no modern fittings and glue smells here.
Stepping up to the door sill takes one over
the port wing root, which is a weak point
on parachuting Rapides. It seems that the
minds of exiting parachutists have no
concern for the delicacy of wooden wing
root structures, as most Rapides used at
some time for this hearty pastime have
wing roots damaged by exuberant para-

chutists' boots, both on embarkation and on departure.

Ducking into the doorway, one confirms the eight dove grey seats for security and the cabin emergency equipment is checked for safe stowage. Then the steep climb up the sloping cabin between the snugly fitting passenger seats takes one to the forward bulkhead, the front face of which the pilot uses as a backrest. What could be called the Captain's Briefing Notice is fixed on the cabin side of the bulkhead. On its ivory surface is printed, in elegant 1930s script: 'Passengers are Requested to return to their Seats on Approaching an Aerodrome and Landing'. That sets a nice period style for the trip.

The immediate impression of the cockpit is of a cramped, angular workspace, with plenty of glazing above, to the sides and ahead. The single pilot's seat is a minimal wooden box, now fitted with a leather back and cushion to match those offered to paying customers. As a token gesture towards safety, a full harness is now fitted, but that's it. No adjustment for height, rake or reach, no armrests, just a nicely covered box with a vestigial backrest. The DH twin transport which followed thirty years after this one has

Left: DH 89A Dragon Rapide G-AEML over the Solent in May 1993, flown by Colin Dodds. This Rapide was built at Hatfield in 1936 as a DH 89, without flaps, and was first flown, by Captain Geoffrey de Havilland, in May that year. It was then delivered to Wrightways of Croydon, for use as their flagship on charter flights across Europe for the next four years. It was rebuilt under the author's guidance beginning in 1988 and flew again in April 1994 after having spent 22 years on the ground. (Geoff Lee)

as the fuel cocks and brake and flap levers, are awkward to operate.

Starting is usually simple, unless the aircraft has not been run for some weeks. With the pre-start checks completed, the starboard engine is primed up to eight times with the little Ki-gass pump on the starboard cockpit wall. All Rapides have electric starters, so after switching on the two magnetos the starter button is pressed until the engine fires. If the weather is cold, simultaneous priming and cranking may be necessary, which means using the right hand to cope with the uncomfortable pumping action and the left to press the starter button, with the knees gripping the central control column to keep the elevators up. The throttles can be left alone. However, most starts are quite straightforward. Now it is time to start the 'three-handed taxying game'.

The aircraft has a castoring tailwheel, a large moment arm between tail and mainwheels and a large keel surface aft of the centre of gravity. It therefore tends to 'weathercock' its nose into the wind, so brakes have to be used on the ground to counter the effect, particularly in a strong wind. Brakes have to be used to steer accurately, but of course they tend to slow the aircraft down, requiring the use of higher and often asymmetric power. Asymmetric power alone can be used for coarse turning control, but this requires considerable anticipation if excessive turning is to be avoided. However, a potential effect of increasing power in certain wind conditions is to allow the tail to rise, and therefore the nose to lower towards the ground. This combination is the dread of all Rapide pilots, who have

Far left: A view seen by thousands of passengers over the sixty-year history of the DH 89. Wiltshire is seen from the front passenger seat of G-AEML in 1993, as are the aircraft's elegant, tapering wings and the many struts and bracing wires. (Ron Smith)

progressed several hundred per cent in terms of the pilot's comfort, but that's what gives this DH model part of its charm.

Around the pilot are spread the means of operating the aircraft, fitted with little apparent thought for their concurrent use on the ground or in the air, being placed more for the convenience of fitting the specialist systems into the airframe. Of course, they can all be reached or seen when required, but not in the most convenient way as with a modern, ergonomic cockpit. While the controls are roughly where you might expect them to be, it is only with practice that they come easily to hand, and some, such

seen photographs of colleagues who 'broke their noses' through letting their tails rise while applying brakes. The Rapide's nose cone crushes as quickly and as easily as its pilot's pride in a 'nose-over'. All this is leading to the question of how to control the manoeuvres on the ground. In light winds the two throttles can be moved independently with the left hand and the control column easily kept in its rear position with the right. Turning can then be controlled by small amounts of differential braking, applied via the rudder pedals. Simple enough.

However, taxying in a crosswind requires the use of the handbrake, which is on the left cockpit floor abeam the pilot's knee and only reached by the left hand, and which must be constantly adjusted to stop the wheels from locking. More modern aircraft make use of control-column brake levers or toe brakes, but not this dear old girl. When the wind is strong, the left hand is needed for constant attention to the throttles to move forward, as well as continuous use of the brake lever to control direction and stopping. If one happens to have only one left hand, then one is forced to use the three-handed method scoffed at by non-Rapide pilots. It works like this. The control which needs the most careful and constant adjustment is the brake lever, low down on the left side, so the left hand is used for constant brake work. The pilot then hunches forward while crooking his right arm around the front of the control column, forcing it rearwards and stretching up to move the two throttle levers on the left sidewall with his right hand. This may explain why all *real* Rapide pilots have hunch-

Above: An indication of the excellent view from the cockpit is given here. The triangular window hinges downwards to give cooling. (Colin Dodds)

backs and gorilla-like right arms. This is one of the trickiest of all aircraft to taxi, but the challenge makes the practice more interesting and it adds to the fun. The rest of the operation is easy, unless one happens to have an engine failure, when the marginal performance again requires delicate hands and feet to maintain accurate speed and balance.

With the simple pre-take-off checks complete, the aircraft is ready. Captain de Havilland's notes tell us that it should use up only 535 yards to reach a height of 50 feet on a maximum-weight take-off, in nil wind, but that target sometimes seems improbable when viewed from the start of a short field. In fact the performance is lively, as the ground roll is short with any sort of headwind. As may be expected with a 1930s design, this aircraft feels most comfortable on grass runways, being skittish on tarmac. The main concern on hard runways is of course the wind direction, which is never right down the middle, so forcing a crosswind technique. With an anticipation of weather-cocking into wind, a combination of a slower than usual opening of the throttles and the careful use of rudders and positive rotation on the ground, the problems inherent in tarmac take-offs will usually be solved.

In this case we are taking off into wind across a gently undulating grass airfield. After the initial application of staggered throttle to counter any torque-induced swing, the Queens settle into a deep, steady bellow, and a check on the gauges indicates their willingness to work. Only small amounts of balancing rudder are needed as the speed builds up, to deter any tendency to swing off course. With the column kept back, then gently towards neutral as the speed increases and the old girl moves across the grass, the Rapide stretches upwards on the undercarriage a couple of times until it flies itself off the ground at around 50 knots, eager to be airborne. The engines are checked again while awaiting the seconds taken to reach the critical single-engine speed of 65 knots. With the safety speed achieved, the pilot can cope with an engine failure and can afford to increase up to his climb speed of 85 knots, which only takes a few more seconds. The controls are nicely effective in the climb, the

heavier ailerons beginning to require more muscle power but the rudders and elevators feeling both light and positive. The Queens need a delicate touch at this point to synchronize engine speeds and so prevent the typical, irritating asynchronous beat which occurs with all propeller twins.

Now safely in its element, the machine feels more comfortable, with both seating and controls better adapted to the airborne phase. Despite the greater feeling of comfort, however, anything over two hours airborne, even in the high-quality leather seats, is something of an ordeal for the pilot sitting on his uphol-

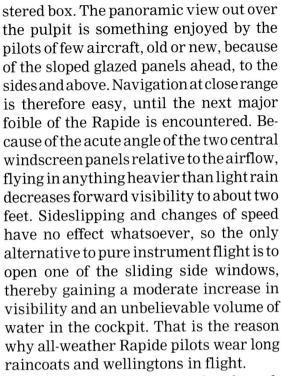

Below: G-AEML at Dunsfold in 1993. Of note here are the high nose angle with the tailwheel on the ground, the large, polished metal spinners containing the mechanism for the De Havilland PD 30 variable-pitch propellers and the Hatfield Town badge on the fin, indicating the aircraft's birthplace. On this early Rapide the fifth port-side cabin window and the short door can be seen; later aircraft had only four windows and a wider cabin door. (Colin Dodds)

stered box. The panoramic view out over the pulpit is something enjoyed by the pilots of few aircraft, old or new, because of the sloped glazed panels ahead, to the sides and above. Navigation at close range is therefore easy, until the next major foible of the Rapide is encountered. Because of the acute angle of the two central windscreen panels relative to the airflow, flying in anything heavier than light rain decreases forward visibility to about two feet. Sideslipping and changes of speed have no effect whatsoever, so the only alternative to pure instrument flight is to open one of the sliding side windows, thereby gaining a moderate increase in visibility and an unbelievable volume of water in the cockpit. That is the reason why all-weather Rapide pilots wear long raincoats and wellingtons in flight.

This is a biplane that needs only moderate balancing rudder in normal turns, unlike most aircraft of its era. Trimming is accurate and sensitive, using the large wheel down by the left knee, which all helps to make the Rapide a stable platform for cruising flights. There is little else to manage in the cruise, except for watching the fuel gauges and adjusting the fuel mixtures when flying above 5,000 feet. With no such equipment as engine cooling cowls, mixture controls or even temperature gauges to worry about, the cruise is usually spent, in inverse proportion, admiring the countryside, navigating, watching the fuel and oil pressure gauges and battling the engines' pervasive de-synchronized mode. This delicate operation, adjusting the throttles and rpm levers if fitted, to keep the engines exactly in tune, is an almost continuous task.

When heading back to base for the more challenging phase, the landing, a quick check of altimeter, engine gauges, fuel levels, radio and the navigation is completed, the throttles are gently retarded to allow the Queens to cool and the nose is lowered for descent. Speed increases, felt and heard by the increased pitch of the flying wires' whistle. The myriad air gaps and holes around the cockpit windows and nose join the chorus, not quite in harmony but at least in unison. This is one of the few 'seat of the pants' transports, which can be flown by sound and feel alone. Descending somewhere just above Middle 'C', which equates to about 120 knots, is comfortable as well as practical, unless there are passengers on board, when a gentler, alto descent is more appropriate. Visibility in good weather is excellent, so a nice tight circuit can be happily flown, using distances slightly greater than those for a Tiger Moth, to cope with the extra speed.

There is a strong wind at the home field on return, so all the way round the circuit a close watch needs to be kept on the airfield windsock's wanderings, to assess the mean speed and direction. In these conditions – very much the sort of weather in which the pioneering Rapide pilots flew their incredibly regular services to the Highlands and Islands – the old aeroplane needs different skills and thought processes from those applied to modern twins.

Despite the pilot's attempts to will the wind into a more convenient westerly direction, it persists in blowing from the north-west, which only allows a short landing run and the choice between two difficult approaches to this small field. The more northerly approach is slightly closer to the general wind direction, but this would need a hop over a 25-foot telephone line running parallel to the stone boundary wall and then straight towards the farm at the other end. The second possibility is to approach on the slightly longer westerly run, about 40 degrees out of wind, so avoiding the high trees on the boundary, then turn sharply into the wind at about twenty feet, within the airfield boundary, for a somewhat longer ground roll. The telephone cable route looks tricky in the strong, gusty wind, so the out-of-wind approach, followed by the last-minute turn into the wind, seems the most practicable.

With the standard fixed-pitch propellers, a good circuit rpm for the Queens is 1,900, which produces around 85 knots at the end of the downwind leg. Aircraft modified with constant-speed propellers need to have their propeller levers adjusted to give 1,900rpm at this point, then the throttles set to match, at about minus three boost. The strong breeze whisks the aircraft rapidly downwind, as the rudimentary downwind check of setting mixtures, fuel contents and brake lever is completed. The touch-down point of the landing strip appears again behind the port lower wing, indicating that it's time to turn on to the final approach.

Throttling back to a gentle 1,200rpm gives around 85 knots in a descending turn, the crosswind skidding the aircraft sideways at a surprising rate, on to final heading. A reminder is needed here not to go below the single-engine safety speed of 65 knots until committed to land, then use is made again of the 'long right arm', to reach down for the flap lever's catch, which is now inconveniently at the top of the lever, way down on the cockpit floor. Flap selection with a tight shoulder harness is impossible in this machine, unless you are an Italian racing driver or an orang-utan. (Alarming oscillations on final approach in Rapides can often be attributed to short-armed pilots attempting to configure the aircraft for landing.)

Turn rate, angle of approach and speed are balanced until the aeroplane is lined up nicely on the selected final approach, allowing for the 40-degree crosswind, at 75 knots and 400 feet. The extra five knots should cover the higher than usual wind and the final turn into wind. Approaching 400 feet, everything looks as expected inside and on the windsock, so commitment to the landing can be made, followed by a speed decrease towards 65 knots at the threshold. The aircraft is very sensitive to gusts and has to be handled carefully near the ground, particularly at slow speeds, as it will readily drop a wing at the stall, especially if asymmetric rudder or power are applied. Normal approaches in calmer conditions are much more friendly, as the aircraft is then smoothly responsive to the controls all the way to touch-down, allowing accurate speed control and judgement of the touch-down point. Rough weather is a different matter.

The wind is obviously causing some turbulence near the ground as, at about 300 feet, the right wing suddenly drops about 30 degrees, prompting a rapid application of full opposite aileron and some rudder to pick up the starboard wing. The aircraft struggles back to an even keel,

Above: A photograph of 'ML's cockpit, taken in 1993, showing the unusual spectacle-shaped control column, which was fitted only to early models. The triangular-topped instrument panel containing the grey-coloured P11 compass is the same as that of the later version but the orange-coloured oil pressure and rpm gauges to the right differ from the original because of this aircraft's modification to embody the more efficient propellers and the VOR indicator (bottom right). Most Rapides in existence today have the 'W'-shaped column. (Colin Dodds)

the speed dies towards a walking pace. Somewhat surprisingly, the Rapide has stopped in less than half the available area, despite the final correcting turn inside the boundary.

With the excitement of the airborne element over, the equally challenging taxying game can be tackled. But first, the 'long right arm' stretches to lock the flap lever in its retracted position, and then the thinking can start on how to cope with crosswind taxying in this breeze. Some speed is kept on for the first part of the turn, and with asymmetric throttle and sparing use of the brakes, and port aileron up, the turn crosswind is started. The manoeuvre works well and the aircraft is soon running downwind, back towards the hangars and safety. After-landing checks are finished on the move as they consist only of checking the flaps up and switching not-needed radios off. On reaching the hangar the old girl is turned into the wind and the trusty Queens are run up to 1,000rpm to cool for a minute. Then it is time to switch off the radios, lights and fuel, then the four engine magnetos, and let the props jerk to a halt. Now the comforting bellow of the Queens has died, the quiet whirring-down of the air-driven gyros is interrupted by the clunk of the brake lever as it is released. The sprightly 60-year-old is once again left to her own silence.

then the turbulence decreases as the ground below smooths out. The direction of approach is working well, and speed is averaging about right as the Rapide crabs into the wind, 40 degrees or so off the final track. Extreme caution is now needed to stop the wind drifting the aeroplane into the high boundary trees on the left as it creeps over the wall, preparing to turn right into the wind. A last look at the speed – 65 over the wall – then right aileron and rudder to skid back into the strong wind's throat. At about 15 feet, wings level, the column can start to come back to decrease the descent rate, throttles brought backwards, and then the aircraft is gently on the grass, level and running nicely, straight into the breeze. There is no need for brakes with this wind, so the tail can come gently down as

For a pilot of a later generation, it is a privilege to accept, in part, the same flying challenges presented to the pioneers of British aviation all those years ago and to be allowed a practical insight into the demands, and the fun, inherent in flying those machines.

Keeping the Dream Alive

Nicholas Veronico

Santa Monica, California's, Clover Field was the birthplace of Douglas Aircraft. Founded in 1922, the Douglas factory eventually came to dominate the north side of the airport. During the Second World War an additional factory was constructed at Long Beach, 30 miles to the south, to handle the volume of aircraft built for the war effort. In the late 1960s all production was moved to Long Beach and Douglas vacated the Clover Field factory in 1972.

Following the closure, the Donald Douglas Museum and Library was established to house the designer's archives. When the airport was 'redeveloped' beginning in the late 1970s the Douglas factory was torn down and replaced with a business park. Developer and warbird collector David Price and others arranged for the construction of an aviation museum on the ramp where the main Douglas buildings once stood, and the assets of the Donald Douglas Museum and Library were acquired and incorporated into the new Museum of Flying.

The Museum of Flying was opened in April 1989 on the historic site of the former

Douglas factory. The contemporary steel and glass building encompasses 53,000 square feet and opens to the airport tarmac, allowing flyable aircraft to be rotated into the museum's display collection. The museum's permanent collection is formed around the milestone aircraft from the Douglas factories. The cornerstone of the collection is the Douglas World Cruiser *New Orleans*.

Douglas had submitted his proposal for the World Cruiser to the Army Air Service on 5 July 1923 and on 1 August the proposal was approved. Four aircraft, named after the major US cities of Seattle, Chicago, Boston, and New Orleans, were delivered by the end of March 1923. The four officially departed from Sand Point, Washington, on a round-the-world flight in the morning of 4 April 1924. *Seattle* crashed on a mountainside but the crew survived after a ten-day trek to civilization. *Boston* made a safe landing in the Atlantic, only to capsize while being towed to the Faeroe Islands. *Chicago* and *New Orleans* went on to fly around the world in 175 days, covering 28,945 miles (46,600km) in 371 hours and 7 minutes of

Below: The Skyraider is one of the Douglas-designed aircraft maintained in airworthy condition by the Museum of Flying. (Nicholas Veronico)

flying time. This epic flight entitled Douglas to adopt as the company's logo the motto 'First Around the World'. Having been built at Clover Field at the same location as the museum, the World Cruiser is a fitting tribute to the early days of Douglas aviation.

Associated with the museum is one of only two airworthy Douglas DC-2s left in the world. Operated and managed by the Douglas Historical Foundation, this important airliner, manufacturer's serial number 1368 and registered as N1394D, was restored to flying condition by a number of Douglas employees. Although based at Long Beach, the DC-2 is flown into Santa Monica for special events. Other aircraft on display include a Curtiss JN-4D Jenny, a Second World War Fairey Swordfish biplane torpedo bomber, a Douglas A-4B Skyhawk painted in the markings of the US Navy's *Blue Angels* aerobatic squadron, a Waco 10 GXE biplane and a Quickie Aircraft Quickie 2.

The museum also boasts a tremendous research library which is accessible, by prior appointment, to visiting authors and historians, and a fully equipped cinema is situated on the third floor, showing classic aviation films and documentaries.

Funding for the museum comes from a number of sources in addition to the nominal admission charges. Special community events hosted at the museum, for example, draw large crowds. The programmes range from displays and sales of 'collectables' and memorabilia to photographic competitions and exhibitions of aviation computer software. The museum can also be hired for special gala events. Thus in 1990 and 1991 it hosted warbird auctions in order to raise funds. Aircraft bought and restored by the museum were sold along with warbirds from private collectors, proceeds from the auc-

tion being placed in a fund to help assure the museum's financial future.

The museum's activities embrace four major areas. First, to compliment the indoor exhibition, a volunteer 'docent' (tour guide) system has been established. Secondly, the museum has a number of flying aircraft which are displayed regularly and maintained in its workshops. These flying aircraft are supported by the third element, the restoration shop volunteers. And finally, in order to vary the museum's display and flying collection, the staff actively search for new acquisitions, including aircraft that need to be recovered from Second World War battlefields.

Helping out with the day-to-day running of the museum is a band of 300 dedicated volunteers who generously give their time assisting in the operations of one of the West Coast's largest aviation

Right: This ex-US Army Hughes OH-6 will soon be receiving attention from the restoration shop volunteers. (Nicholas Veronico)

Left: The museums's volunteers restored this Lockheed T-33 Shooting Star to static display condition. (Nicholas Veronico)

displays. Areas of the volunteers' responsibilities include acting as 'docents'; looking after the museum's membership and public relations; acting as speakers to take the museum's message to the outside world; operating the cinema; conducting historical research; producing publications; organizing air shows and local events; undertaking clerical duties; and staffing the museum's gift shop.

The docents comprise some sixty to seventy active volunteers who lead tours through the museum. During such a tour a visitor will spend half an hour in the theatre watching films on current and historic aviation subjects, and this is followed by a walking tour of the museum where over 150 displays are set up. 'In order to be a good volunteer, all someone needs is the desire to do it,' says Bernie Bernard, a retired Air Force colonel and one of the volunteer co-ordinators. 'That's all they need because we can find a place anywhere in the system for them to do what they like to do. Some don't know what they want to do, so we try them out in different areas.'

The docents are the foundation of the volunteer system. They have to learn a lot of things: they have to know something about every aircraft in the building; they have to know about all the displays; they have to have a good speaking presence; and they have to like people. 'You have to have some actor and some comedian in you to hold a group's attention for an hour and a half,' says Bernard.

Potential docents are given on-the-job training; they do not have to have an extensive knowledge of aviation when they start since the museum will teach them. New docents take home a package of written material, including guidebooks detailing every aircraft in the collection and the museum's displays. Then they are paired with an experienced docent, following his or her tour to see 'how it is done'. Docents also work during special evening events and weekend fly-ins. 'We keep a list that tells where the airplanes are,' explains Bernard. 'Because our planes fly, that means they are in maintenance at some point in time and you may not see the P-51D *Cottonmouth* or the Spitfires. They may be here, or at the maintenance hangar, or they may be off site at an air show. There are people who come here only to see the Spitfires, or the Hurricane, or a Mustang. And they are very

Fly Past, Fly Present

disappointed if they are not here. So if they call up, we have this list available to tell them.'

Docents complete this list. They also run tours of the restoration hangar for adults. 'Within the corps of volunteers, whatever is done in any major corporation, that same job exists here from a volunteer standpoint,' says volunteer co-ordinator Margie Rohan. 'The volunteers that we have have so many talents . . . that it would be impossible for any one corporation to buy this talent. The talent that is here is absolutely awesome. I wanted to come here because I live in Santa Monica – I'm close. This is my community museum and I wanted to give something back to the community. Volunteers are giving their most precious commodity, which is their own time.'

'I learned to fly right here at Clover Field when I was twelve years old,' says Bernard. 'I used to hang around here. I was a "gofer": I'd "go for" anything to get an airplane ride. Unfortunately kids nowadays cannot hang out at the airport, so bringing them to the museum is the best way to expose them to aviation.'

A second side of the museum brings history to life, and flying, maintaining and restoring Second World War aircraft is a major attraction for the museum. Each year a number of aircraft, the restoration shop's mechanics and some volunteers travel to the National Championship Air Races held at Reno, Nevada's, Stead Field. Here the museum's P-51D Mustangs are put through their paces, flying at speeds in excess of 400mph around a nine-mile closed racing course.

The museum's collection of British aircraft is a big draw at air shows. Two Spitfires, a Mk IX (N930LB) and a Mk XIV (N749DP), and a Hurricane XII (N678DP)

Right: Cottonmouth *is one of three flyable P-51D Mustangs housed at the museum. (Nicholas Veronico)*

are maintained in flying condition by the museum; at the time of writing, the Hurricane is thought to be the only flying example of its type in North America. Completing the collection of airworthy aircraft are a Douglas A1-H (AD-6) Skyraider and a North American T-28, both of which are flown at most of the southern California air shows.

The Museum of Flying's Director of Restoration and Maintenance, Bruce Lockwood, oversees the fleet of flyable aircraft. His shops can do anything required to maintain a Second World War aircraft, from general maintenance through 50- and 100-hour inspections, annual inspections and engine changes to complete restorations. Lockwood and

Left: The museum's Hawker Hurricane undergoes an inspection in the restoration hangar. *(Nicholas Veronico)*

his staff are currently putting the finishing touches to an F8F-1 Bearcat. The Bearcat was the last piston-engine design built by Grumman.

A second group of volunteers works in the museum's restoration shops, where aircraft or major assemblies such as cockpits are prepared for display, hangar work such as building shipping and storage crates is undertaken and parts for aircraft restorations are organized. To get involved, a person must first express an interest to a member of the staff – which is easily done. One can talk to a docent during a tour, contact the museum on the telephone or call in person, find out when the work days are scheduled and show up ready to help out.

Many volunteers are recruited by word of mouth. 'Usually we set up an orientation with our new volunteers,' says Kurt Stricklen, the museum's maintenance and restoration co-ordinator who supervises the restoration shop volunteers. 'We show them the layout of the shop and what different projects we have in the works. Our staff try to find a volunteer's strong points and we start them in that area. We have a core of about sixty volunteers working in hangar. One volunteer who lives in Laguna (about 100 miles from the museum), Bobby Altman, drives every day to the Orange County Airport and flies her Cessna 150 to Santa Monica five days a week. That's dedication!'

What are the minimum requirements for a volunteer? Stricklen says that age doesn't matter, but one must have the desire to be around old aeroplanes and want to get dirty: 'A lot of the work is just clean-up – cleaning parts, wire-brushing parts, painting, stripping. Ninety-nine per cent of the time volunteers will work on the non-flying static aircraft and displays. The flying aircraft require licensed airframe and powerplant mechanics – although quite often some of our volunteers who have worked here for a long time will assist the A&Ps. We like people who really have an interest in old planes and realize that most of this work is taking something apart and remembering how it goes together, building new parts and cleaning up existing ones.'

The majority of the shop equipment has been donated by southern Californian aerospace and machinery companies. The restoration facility has a welding area equipped for both Tig and gas welding; a 'clean room' used to store small parts and projects that cannot be disturbed when not being worked on; the usual variety of bench tools, including grinders, sanders, surfacers, a drill press and bead blast cabinets for removing paint and light corrosion; a solvent tank; an electrical section for aircraft wiring and testing; a sheet metal shop outfitted with sheet metal breaks, rollers, shears, shrinkers, stretchers, punches and a large press break; a drafting table; and a machine shop run by Jarvis Williams, a retired machinist who makes just about anything the restoration team could need.

Volunteers used every asset in the museum's shops when they assisted in the replacement of a Lockheed P-38 Lightning's reconnaissance nose section. Metalsmith Phil Greenburg, with the assistance of many volunteers, reconstructed from plans a fighter gun nose for the P-38. This project took months, but, once it was completed, no one could tell the difference between a stock gun nose and the replacement built from scratch by the museum's craftsmen. Some of the smaller projects that have gone through the restoration shop and have been completed by volunteers include a number of engine cutaways, a Beech 18 cockpit and a T-33 Shooting Star cockpit simulator. These projects can be seen on display in the museum and show the high standard of work put out by the volunteers. Major projects recently completed and now on display are a Fokker Triplane replica and a complete T-33. The 1950s-era jet trainer arrived disassembled and needing lots of work. The volunteers cleaned the aircraft,

Right: Manufacturing a 'gun nose' for a P-38. This Lightning arrived at the museum with a photo-reconnaissance nose, but the classic Second World War look was preferred. The aircraft later sold for $1.5 million at auction. (Michael Burr)
Below: The finished product. This is how the P-38 appeared when the gun nose was completed – authentic in every detail. (Nicholas Veronico)

mated the wings to the fuselage and then began the restoration process to static display standards. Many small parts, access doors and fairings were built from scratch to replace missing parts. The aircraft was painted and is now displayed outdoors at the museum. Stricklen plans to have the volunteers clean up the T-33's Allison J33 jet engine for a display inside the museum.

The volunteers are also justifiably proud of the Bell P-39Q Airacobra they have restored. This aircraft, serial number 42-1993, was accepted by the Army Air Force on 8 June 1943 and served in the South Pacific with the Seventh Air Force's 82nd Tactical Reconnaissance Squadron in the New Guinea theatre. The tricycle-gear Bell fighter features automobile-style doors and a 1,200-horsepower Allison V-1710-85 twelve-cylinder, liquid-cooled engine mounted amidships behind the pilot's seat. It was armed with a single 37mm cannon which fired through the propeller hub, two .50-calibre machine guns mounted in the upper cowling and four .30-calibre machine guns mounted in the wing. Bell constructed 9,558 Airacobras during the war.

Like most of the projects assigned to the volunteers, the P-39Q arrived disassembled, and it still carried some of its original Second World War markings: on the nose was 'Brooklyn Bum 2nd' and behind the cockpit was 'Syracuse NY',

Right: One of the museum's P-51s races each year at the National Championships held during September at Reno, Nevada. The highly modified Dago Red *is a former Unlimited Gold Race winner. (Nicholas Veronico)*

while the pilot's entry door featured a green four-leaf clover in a yellow circle plus nine bomb mission marks and the name of the pilot, Lieutenant Peter A. McDermott. Volunteers laid the parts out to resemble an aircraft. Next, the empennage was attached to the fuselage. The wings were in poor shape at best. The tyres were frozen, retracted into the wheel wells, the wing spars had begun to de-

laminate and the surface sheet metal was heavily corroded.

The first major hurdle was to free the landing gear and attach the wings to the fuselage. Once this was accomplished, the P-39 sat on its own gear and truly resembled a fighter. The wing spars were stabilized and the skins were treated or replaced. Next, all missing inspection panels and landing gear doors were fabri-

Left: A Japanese Zero fighter laid out in the restoration hangar. The tail of a Spitfire Mk IX undergoing maintenance is visible in the foreground. (Michael Burr)
Right: The tail section of the Zero under restoration, showing the ribs and longerons. Note the Indonesian graffiti on the tail. (Michael Burr)

cated. The volunteers primed the aircraft for paint and when the Airacobra emerged from the paint shop it looked fantastic. Twelve dedicated volunteers, with occasional assistance from the museum's expert mechanics, had completed the restoration to display standards in only five months.

Currently the volunteers are restoring a B-29 cockpit section. This is expected to be a three-year project, and everything must be reconstructed or acquired for this restoration. When the museum received the nose it was just a hulk, and volunteers are re-manufacturing instrument panels, control panels, sticks, yokes, hydraulics and wiring. 'We are planning to restore a number of cock-

pit sections which we will mount to the museum's exterior walls', explains Stricklen, 'so kids can walk in them and get a "hands-on" feel for what it is like to sit in the pilot's seat. The B-29 cockpit will be the centrepiece for this display.' Next on the volunteers' list of projects will be the restoration to static display standards of an ex-US Army Hughes OH-6 scout helicopter, a UH-1 Huey helicopter and a Convair T-29 cockpit.

Taking the lead in aircraft recovery and restoration, the museum recently acquired a number of rare Japanese aircraft from the former battlefields of the Pacific. A Mitsubishi G4M1 'Betty' bomber, a Kawasaki Ki-61 Hien ('Tony') fighter and a Yokusuka D4Y Suisei

('Judy') dive bomber plus an A6M2 Model 33 were discovered by aviation historian Bruce Fenstermaker on an island off the coast of Indonesia. Although the aircraft were stripped and had sat abandoned on the island for 46 years, they were in fairly good condition, deemed 'restorable' by Bruce Lockwood.

A Mitsubishi A6M2 Model 21 (folding wing-tips) Zero arrived at the museum first. It is currently under restoration as a long-term project. Plans call for the installation of an original 1,130-horsepower Nakajima NK1C Sakae 12, fourteen-cylinder radial engine. The museum has acquired a number of derelict engines and they feel that one running example can be built up. The Model 21 was recovered along with the cockpit section of a second Zero. When its restoration is complete it will become the second Zero flying with its original powerplant, joining The Air Museum/Planes of Fame's A6M5 Model 52 at Chino, California.

The Ki-61 Hien or Swallow (Allied code-name 'Tony') appears to be in the roughest condition. The tail is separated behind the cockpit, a practice instituted by the US Army and Navy at the end of the war to prevent aircraft from flying. Many sheetmetalmen feel that this is not a major setback in a restoration project as the tail section has to be de-mated from the fuselage during the rebuild anyway. One unusual feature of this Ki-61 is that it does retain the armour plate for its pilot's seat.

Above: The museum's Mitsubishi 'Betty' bomber is one of the most complete examples preserved today. This restoration will be a major undertaking for the museum. (Nicholas Veronico)

Right: *The Convair T-29 cockpit section has had its skin brightened and the interior is next on the project list. (Nicholas Veronico)*

The 'Tony' is powered by a licence-built copy of the German Daimler-Benz DB-601A inverted V-12 liquid-cooled engine, one of which was recovered with the aircraft. The Hien was an excellent fighter, but it was built in insufficient numbers to help turn the tide of the air war. However, it was not matched in combat by the Allies until the introduction of the P-51 Mustang.

The Mitsubishi G4M1 'Betty' bomber symbolized Japanese naval air power. It launched strikes against the Philippines in the first days of the war and also carried the surrender party to Ie Shima in September 1945. Admiral Yamamoto lost his life in a 'Betty' over the island of Bougainville on 18 April 1943 when his aircraft was intercepted and destroyed by a flight of Lockheed P-38s. This example is about 75 per cent complete and is only the second 'Betty' in the hands of a museum; the National Air and Space Museum has a 'Betty' cockpit and tail turret. Carrying a crew of seven, the G4M1 was armed with four 7.7mm machine guns in the dorsal, right and left waist and nose positions and one 20mm cannon in the tail turret. A total of 2,446 'Bettys' were constructed during the war. The museum's aircraft currently rests on its belly in a storage hangar. It appears that the G4M-1 may have crash-landed as the lower section of the bombardier's nose compartment is missing and one engine seems to be feathered.

The museum's Yokosuka D4Y Suisei or Comet (Allied code-name 'Judy') is only the second of its type to be recovered from the battlefields of the Pacific, another having been found on Yap in the Caro-lines. Following a lengthy restoration the 'Judy' is now displayed at the Yasukuni Shrine in Tokyo. The D4Y-1 first flew in December 1940. It featured a retractable undercarriage and an internal bomb bay capable of carrying 1,234lb of bombs, and it was equipped with two wing-mounted 7.7mm machine guns and one rearward-firing 7.92mm machine gun. The aircraft had a maximum speed of 343mph at 15,585 feet. A total of 2,038 D4Ys of all types were constructed. The museum's acquisition of rare Japanese combat aircraft represents a major contribution to the preservation of a number of hitherto 'extinct' aircraft types.

The Yak-3 was an outstanding air superiority fighter at altitudes below 20,000 feet. Armed with a 37mm cannon firing through the propeller hub and two 20mm cannon mounted above the cowling, the aircraft packed a formidable punch. In early 1944 the Yakovlev design bureau tested an improved, all-metal Yak-3U, earlier Yak-3s having been equipped with wooden wings and tail sections. Nearly half a century later, in 1991, the bureau loaned the Museum of Flying an original Soviet Second World War Yak-3 fighter for display. Following on from this has been one of the most exciting projects ever undertaken by an aviation museum. During the museum's second auction in October 1992 it was announced that new production aircraft would be built in the same factory from the same tooling as the original Yak-3s. These aircraft are being built to the all-metal Yak-3U specifications and will feature a V-12 Allison V-1710 liquid-cooled engine. Designated Yak-3UA, and selling for $495,000

apiece, only twenty airframes are planned to be constructed; one has been completed, and this was displayed at the 1993 Paris *Salon*.

Future plans for the museum call for the cockpit sections currently under restoration to be enclosed in a courtyard. This area will give visitors the opportunity to explore the cockpits of aircraft from single-engine, general-aviation types to airliners and the massive B-29 Superfortress. A Douglas DC-3 with an executive interior has also been acquired and the museum hopes to operate it on an FAA Part 91 charter basis, giving aerial tours of Santa Monica, Malibu and other scenic southern Californian locales. After the priority volunteer projects have

been completed, a decision will be made as to whether the museum's volunteer staff will tackle the restoration to static display standard of the recently recovered Kawasaki Ki-61 'Tony' fighter.

The Museum of Flying is located at the Santa Monica Airport at 2772 Donald Douglas Loop North, Santa Monica, California 95405, telephone (310) 392-8822. The Museum is closed on Mondays and Tuesdays and is open from 10 a.m. to 5 p.m. from Wednesday to Sunday.

No matter where you live there is an aviation museum nearby. Support these museums by taking their tours and donating to their preservation funds. Best of all, donate your time and talents to preserving aviation history.

Warbird World

Paul Coggan

During the 1980s the warbird scene changed dramatically. In 1980 there were a handful of people rebuilding warbirds and only a small number of full-time professional companies rebuilding complete airframes in the United Kingdom, though the United States had many more firms involved in this kind of work. In Britain in the 1990s the story is very different, with some six full-time professional rebuilding concerns supported by a well planned and generally lucrative warbirds industry.

To illustrate the growth in the rebuilding of vintage fighters, we will take a single type, the Supermarine Spitfire. In 1980 there were some 25 airworthy Spitfires, but in 1994 there were over 40, with another fifteen being rebuilt to fly, some as commercial projects being worked on full-time by professional companies but many more being reconstructed – principally as a hobby – as long-term ventures.

The main British companies rebuilding Spitfires are Trent Aero, resident at East Midlands Airport; Dick Melton Aviation, at Micheldever in Hampshire; Historic Flying, at Audley End Airfield in Essex; and Airframe Assemblies, based in the Isle of Wight. Such is the interest in and demand for these warbirds that these concerns – especially Historic Flying – have a number of aircraft on their books and many more waiting to be rebuilt. They are supported by a multitude of smaller firms constructing major and minor sub-assemblies and larger units such as wings. On the Isle of Wight, as part of a range of aviation manufacturing activities, Steve Vizard's Airframe Assemblies are rebuilding Spitfire wings and, over the years, have turned out many such units for customers in Britain, the USA, Australia and New Zealand.

There are also a large number of specialist engine rebuilders, tackling anything from Rolls-Royce Merlins (mainly for Spitfires and Mustangs), through large American radials and British sleeve-valve engines, to the more specialist power-plants like the German DB 605. It is ironic that the majority of Merlin engine rebuilders are located in the United States. All produce high-quality work to feed the thirst of the airframe companies. In Cali-

Right, upper: The start of a project, in this case an ex-Indian Air Force Spitfire Mk XVIII in Rudy Frasca's hangar at Champaign, Illinois. This is the second Spitfire that Frasca is rebuilding in the United States; the first is now airworthy, having been rebuilt partly in the US, whereupon it was shipped to Audley End in Britain. Historic Flying then completed, painted and flight-tested the aircraft, following which it was dismantled and shipped back across the Atlantic. (Paul Coggan/Warbirds Worldwide)

Right, lower: High-backed Spitfire Mk XVI TB252 was rescued from RAF Bentley Priory where it had served as a gate guardian. It is scheduled to be rebuilt by Historic Flying in early 1995 for a German customer. (Paul Coggan/Warbirds Worldwide)

fornia, for example, there are several specialist engine refurbishing companies, including Mike and Kim Nixon's Vintage V-12s and Jack Hovey's Hovey Machine Products. In Minnesota, JRS Enterprises (founded by the late Jack Sandberg and now run by his daughter Janet) have overhauled many Merlins, Allisons and larger radials over the years and their services are very much in demand across the world. At Fort Wayne Air Service, Baer Field, Indiana, John E. Dilley oversees Merlin overhaul for selected customers who also have their Mustangs based at the facility. Dwight Thorn (Mystery Air Division) specializes in Merlins for racing aircraft and has been involved in this activity for many years. A 'zero-timed' Merlin can cost up to $75,000 and the time between overhauls varies enormously. In Britain, Aviation Jersey have been the main Merlin and Griffon rebuilders, and CFS Aeroproducts, a new company, are just launching a major Pratt & Whitney engine rebuilding facility near Coventry Airport, where the main customer is Air Atlantique, who operate nine DC-3s for freight-hauling and oil-spraying.

In the 1990s, flying and maintaining a warbird is an expensive business. Merlins are still readily available, though their condition varies. Parts like crankshafts are in shorter supply, but it is only as matter of time before someone obtains the relevant aviation authority approval and begins to manufacture these from scratch, so giving the Merlin, and Merlin-powered aircraft, a new lease of life.

There are also companies specializing in airframe components – sheet metal, CNC-engineered and cast. There is even a

British company – Butser Rubber, located in Hampshire – which manufactures large and small rubber components, utilizing equivalent modern materials to strict CAA requirements.

Rebuilding a Spitfire is a complex operation. The aircraft can be considered, broadly, as four units, fuselage (including empennage and tail surfaces, mainplanes (wings, including control surfaces), engine (including propeller) and systems, the latter encompassing literally all the bits and pieces, from rubber fittings through instruments, navigation equipment and controls to the oxygen system. Most people will be familiar with the need to have the aircraft's many thousands of rivets replaced owing to the high magnesium content of the originals and their consequent corrosion.

It is generally accepted that much of the original airframe will have to be replaced – often as much as 60 per cent, sometimes more – including the wing spars, which have to be machined. A batch of spars was manufactured in the late 1970s, and a company called Microscan Engineering, at Long Eaton near Nottingham, is able to undertake this task as well as making undercarriage and other vital components to special order. Both the fuselage and the wings have to be jigged, since when the skins are removed the structural integrity of the airframe has to be maintained. The fuselage, after every component has been stripped out to leave the basic shell, is jigged in a heavy structure often bolted to the floor and aligned using lasers for maximum accuracy, and the rivets are drilled out. Castings are non-destructive tested or x-rayed, al-

Left: Seen here in a specially built jig at Rayne in Essex is low-backed Spitfire Mk XVI RW382, also rescued from the gate of an RAF station. The manufacture of the jig, utilizing Supermarine drawings and some very accurate instrumentation, ensures not only that the fuselage is straight but also that the structure is correctly rebuilt.
Above: Horizontal stabilizer on rebuild.
Right: Tail cone and fin, also jigged before the skins were removed and the internal structure cleaned up and prepared for the new metal covering. (All photos: Paul Coggan/ Warbirds Worldwide)

though quite often the fuselage ribs can be re-used ('will go again', in the parlance of the trade). Old metal skin panels can be used as a pattern for new ones, which are formed (i.e., rolled, shaped and hammered) and then painted before being pinned to the overhauled and re-assembled fuselage frames and riveted in place. A similar but more complex operation is performed on the wings, which are jigged vertically, leading edge to the floor. The wing structure contains awkward assemblies like the undercarriage and fuel tanks. Premier Fuel Systems at Castle Donington undertake the manufacture of new Spitfire fuel cells. Their main business is producing custom fuel cells for Formula 1 racing cars and the Spitfire units are built to exacting standards, with many fire-retardant properties.

Once the basic fuselage shell is complete, the fitting of systems, including all the electrics, can commence. Many owners follow today's trend of rebuilding the aircraft to 'stock' configuration, that is, to the same condition as when it first left a factory, given that modern safety measures have to be observed and that even a vintage aircraft requires up-to-date navigational equipment in today's crowded airspace. This equipment is often skilfully hidden in the most inventive places, and even the gun bays form small compartments for light luggage. A minority of owners choose more modern-looking, ergonomically perfect cockpits finished in light grey, but some prefer a balance of the externally authentic and the internally modern, suited for flying in the 1990s. More often than not, the latest radios and oxygen systems are fitted.

Far left, upper: The cockpit under rebuild. Not only does the cockpit have to be completely stripped out and cleaned, with items replaced where necessary, more often than not the owner will require a totally authentic appearance, right down to the colour specifications for the interior paintwork. (Paul Coggan/Warbirds Worldwide)

Far left, lower: Spitfire Mk XVIII seat. The rebuilding of this item, which has to stand the pressures of everyday wear and stress, is a project in itself. One Spitfire owner in Britain found himself in trouble when his seat collapsed during an aerobatic sequence. There could have been a disaster, but apart from an injured back and a much lower position than normal for landing he suffered no ill-effects. (Paul Coggan/Warbirds Worldwide)

Below: A magic moment. Some of the first engine running trials for this Spitfire Mk XVI took place in March 1991. The engine was rebuilt in the United States, where it was bench-tested and the screens pulled to check for metal. It was then packed and shipped to Britain, where, once installed and hooked up to the systems, it underwent extensive ground running trials at various power settings, with the aircraft's tail lashed firmly to the ground. A few weeks later, when the engine had been given the all-clear and any minor snags had been cured, the aircraft was cowled up and flown for the first time. (Paul Coggan/Warbirds Worldwide)

By now the fuselage and wings have been removed from their jigs, and after the systems have been installed and the aircraft plumbed for hydraulics and electrics the two main components are mated together and the systems linked up. At this point the engine is usually installed. In most cases the engine rebuilders will have bench-tested the Merlin (or, in later marks of the aircraft, the Griffon) for between two and four hours. Once the engine has been installed, the propeller is fitted. By now exhaustive undercarriage retraction tests will have been completed, and the engine will be test-run again for many hours until the rebuilders are happy that the engine and systems are functioning in unison as they should be. Ground running is almost a religion, with temperatures and pressures constantly checked, screens pulled

to discover whether there are any tell-tale signs of metal in the oil and coolant pipes checked for leaks.

The wooden Spitfire propeller is a story in itself. During the war there were many propeller manufacturers in Great Britain, but 1994 sees only one still able to produce this marvellous piece of equipment. However, again ironically, the Spitfire propeller is manufactured by Hoffman in Germany, although the United Kingdom agents Skycraft and the very enthusiastic Michael Barnett are always close to the action when these units are being made. Although a detailed account of propeller manufacturing is well beyond the scope of this feature, it is a long and interesting process and, in common with other aspects of Spitfire refurbishment, one which makes full use of up-to-date technology.

All this activity has to be meticulously checked by the Civil Aviation Authority, and each piece on the aircraft, down to the very last rivet, nut and bolt, has to be approved as aviation-released material. This of course brings about a mountain of paperwork and correspondence, with the accompanying expense. Generally, the CAA inspector attached to a particular project makes many visits during the course of a rebuild, each component or stage in the work being signed off by a CAA licensed engineer and again signed off as having been approved by the CAA inspector. At the time of writing a new system of certification is being introduced by the CAA, though as few facts are available it would be inappropriate to comment on its likely effectiveness.

At this stage of the proceedings the aircraft is usually painted, and of all the ingredient parts of a successful rebuild it is this one which often attracts the most criticism from enthusiasts! The owner, having spent a considerable amount of time and effort, not to mention money, in seeing his pride and joy made ready to take to the air, is now faced with the unenviable task of selecting a scheme. Some choose custom finishes. Spencer Flack had his Spitfire XIV painted bright red and attracted a mass of complaints. (In all honesty, the writer feels that it made a refreshing change, and, after all, if one owns a Spitfire one is surely entitled to choose the colours it wears!) The majority of owners favour authentic schemes, however. One talented individual, a perfectionist well versed in the application of accurate schemes utilizing modern paints, is Clive Denney. Thor-

Left, upper: The engine matches the airframe: Mike Nixon at Vintage V-12s in California completely rebuilt this Merlin engine for Eddie Coventry's low-back Spitfire Mk XVI TD248. (Paul Coggan/ Warbirds Worldwide)
Left, lower: Another Merlin, this one sitting in its stand awaiting a rebuild. (Paul Coggan/ Warbirds Worldwide)
Right: Putting the tail unit on to Spitfire Mk IX TE566. Quite a job, but once the bolt holes and attachment points are lined up – hey presto! (Paul Coggan/ Warbirds Worldwide)

ough research and experience go into painting warbirds, and Denney has undertaken more assignments of this nature than most, producing all the right shades, all the correct markings and even the most minor stencils. It does make a difference, and many enthusiasts can spot a Denney paint job at 100 yards!

Once all the paperwork is in order and the aircraft has been tested as much as possible on the ground, it is time to apply for a permit to fly it. At this point still more testing is carried out, to ensure that the aircraft will perform as it should. C of G calculations guarantee that the aircraft is correctly balanced. It should be borne in mind that today's Spitfires are generally lighter than the aircraft of the 1940s in that they do not carry armament or armour plate, which while vital fifty years ago are no longer required. Once the CAA is satisfied that the aircraft has been rebuilt in accordance with the rules and is ready to fly, an experienced pilot is scheduled to perform the 10-hour test programme, again to CAA requirements. Very often this is where the real work starts: test-flying shows up the slightest imperfection, and, as all British rebuilders are perfectionists, each and every snag has to be ironed out.

Following the first flight there is generally much celebration, the majority of the engineers involved having been working very hard, often for a number of years, towards the goal of seeing the aircraft take to the air. What started off as a loose arrangement of components has been

Left: All cowled up and ready to be flown: Spitfire RW382, first off the line at Historic Flying, Audley End. (Paul Coggan/ Warbirds Worldwide)

transformed into the classic shape of a Spitfire. Those graceful lines look superb, more so in the air than ever they can on the ground in a dusty museum. For many, including the writer, the excitement is as much in seeing the aircraft being skilfully rebuilt as in watching it perform aerobatics against an azure sky. The smell of metal, oil, leather and jointing compound mixed in with dope – heady days!

Mention must now be made of the owners, that dedicated bunch of individuals who make all this possible. The writer declines to give a blanket figure as to what a Spitfire might be worth – each individual aircraft is different – but suffice it to say that to rebuild even a complete aircraft to flying condition can cost up to £500,000. Operating costs are not for the faint-hearted: £3,000 an hour including fuel and insurance is a typical figure. Is it worth it? Though, like every other

activity, the vintage aircraft market has suffered as a result of the recession of the 1990s, many compare it to the classic car market – incorrectly in the writer's opinion. There is no comparison, for the rewards are higher and the number of aircraft (and therefore of owners) lower. One thing is certain: at the time of writing warbirds are increasing in value, and flyable aircraft in numbers.

So, one might ask, where did all these Spitfires come from in the first place? There had to be a starting point for each and every rebuild. Put simplistically, after the Second World War the Spitfire was either retired or hived off to foreign air forces. Several of the former RAF aircraft were dispatched for use as ground instructional airframes or as gate guardians, while air arms such as those of India, Italy, Israel, Belgium and Ireland all took delivery of Spitfires, and many of

Below: Jack Bourret's P-51D, based in southern France, is named Jumpin' Jacques. *The aircraft was rescued from South America, where it had been based for a number of years. (Paul Coggan/Warbirds Worldwide)*

them survive today after a chequered history and a host of owners. Undoubtedly the most prolific collector of Spitfires in recent years was Doug Arnold of Warbirds of Great Britain, who, at the peak of his collecting days, had ten aircraft. He made several trips to India, where he bought a number of airframes, and at one time there was a healthy Spitfire production line at Blackbushe in Hampshire. Arnold died fairly recently and many of his Spitfires had been traded for equally interesting aircraft, but his collection, though now dispersed, remains intact.

More recently the Ministry of Defence decided that they should withdraw all the Spitfires (and Hurricanes) from duty as gate guardians, where they were at the mercy of the weather, and put them into store. The idea was that the aircraft would be traded against a 'wants' list, mainly of aircraft for the RAF Museum. Many such trades have now been made, and the result is a healthier population of airworthy Spitfires and a number of hitherto unobtainable aircraft available for display at Hendon.

Though Doug Arnold was the first person to trade a gate-guarding Spitfire with the MoD, one enterprising person, Tim Routsis (now a Director of Historic Flying at Audley End), came to an arrangement whereby he supplied several GRP Spitfires and Hurricanes as well as a P-40 for five gate guardians. To date, four of these aircraft have been put back into

the air, and Historic Flying are now hard at work on their tenth Spitfire rebuild. Several other individuals have roamed the world in search of Spitfire airframes, including Robert Lamplough, who visited Israel on several occasions in the early 1970s and recovered many historic airframes for rebuilding.

As related earlier, what was once a 'cottage industry' has now grown considerably, and whilst the rebuilding of warbirds is still a very small part of the world's aviation industry as a whole it is one of the most exciting. No doubt for many people the activities of the 1990s are the most exhilarating. With the ending of the Cold War and the demolition of the Berlin Wall has come a veritable flood of warbirds. Following the end of hostilities on the Eastern Front at the end of the Second World War, many of the battlefields became prohibited areas for civilians. For obvious reasons, large regions of the Soviet wilderness were strewn with German, American and British warplanes. The Luftwaffe had fought extensively over the Eastern Front, and, with the thaw in relations between East and West and the opening up of these vast tracts, a number of exciting aircraft have been discovered. The two most significant have been a Focke Wulf FW 190, which is being rebuilt in Europe, and a Curtiss P-40B, rescued by Stephen Grey of The Fighter Collection. After the P-40 was recovered it was sent to Britain to be surveyed. The early Allison engine was then sent on to JRS Enterprises in Minneapolis and has been rebuilt and tested prior to its re-installation, and the fuselage and wings have also been dis-

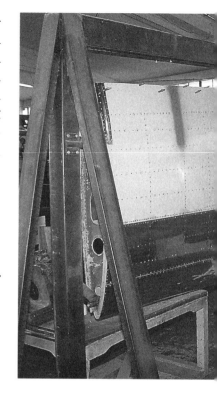

patched to the United States for rebuilding. Once complete, the aircraft will join another P-40 which is being reconstructed in Russia. Many other P-40s have been recovered, the majority originating in Lend-Lease contracts and some bearing RAF serials. Also of note have been several Messerschmitt Bf 110s, two of which have gone to the Alpine Fighter Collection of Sir Tim Wallis at Wanaka in New Zealand. A handful of Hurricanes have also been recovered.

Whilst these finds have been a far cry from the rumoured 'Hurricanes in crates in scrapyards', they have the makings of flyable aircraft. The FW 190 and P-40B in particular were remarkably complete, as were some of the Bf 110s. The German airframes discovered in Russia also include a number of Bf 109s, some taken from lakes and others from forests. Some of the relics were further damaged during their recovery, but this has been as a result of the Russians' inexperience in moving such remains safely rather than vandalism. One Bf 110 is reported to have been dropped while being lifted by helicopter from the tundra.

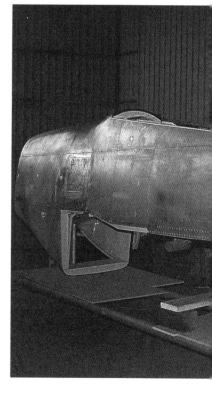

Not only are wrecks being recovered: there is also great activity surrounding the manufacture of replica warplanes. Several companies in Russia are re-manufacturing Second World War-era fighters, including the Yakovlev bureau with a limited run of Yak-3s. These aircraft are much sought after by collectors. Capel Aviation in France are involved in a project with a Romanian aircraft manufacturer to build ten Yak-11s. Alain Capel is the Frenchman who masterminded the recovery of some 42 Yak-18s from the Egyptian Air Force in the late 1970s. All these airframes sold, and most are now airworthy. A large number were rebuilt using their original Shvetsov engines, but some fly with American powerplants. The Yak-11 has gained a remarkable reputation as a high-performance warbird. When the ex-Egyptian aircraft were sold they went for $25,000; today, very much in demand, they can fetch up to $200,000.

No feature on warbirds would be worthwhile without mention being made of the North American Mustang. The P-51 is to the Americans what the Spitfire is to the British. It is the most prolific, and also the most sought-after, warbird in the world and no serious collection is complete without one. Despite a small drop in the prices of warbirds during the 1990s recession, the P-51 has hardly suffered, thanks largely to the constant demand for flyable airframes.

The Mustang is surrounded by a powerful rebuilding industry. At Chino in California, a company called Pioneer Aero has a massive stock of Mustang spares and components, and those parts that are no longer available 'off the shelf' are being re-manufactured using extensive tool-

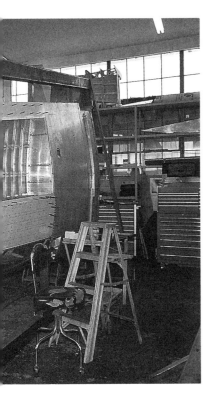

Left, upper: Chino, California: an ex-Dominican Air Force Mustang at Steve Hinton's Fighter Rebuilders, for the late Jack Sandberg. Sandberg had been involved with warbirds for tens of years and wanted this aircraft perfect in every way. Platinum Plus was completely reskinned and a highly polished natural metal surface was the result. (Paul Coggan/Warbirds Worldwide)
Left, lower: Mustang fuselage at Pioneer Aero, also at Chino. Pioneer specialize in P-51s, and two-seat TF-51s. So far they have built up four aircraft, all to exceptionally high standards. (Paul Coggan/Warbirds Worldwide)

ing. Pioneer have been responsible for the production of many airframes from genuine P-51 parts, including two dual-control TF-51s – important aircraft for training pilots new to the type. At Kissimmee in Florida there is even a company providing a full Mustang training programme. Stallion 51 Corporation operate a TF-51 full time, providing a variety of formal flight training courses, and are able to provide an FAA Letter of Authorization to fly the type. The company also have a ground school and have been contracted by the US Navy to provide a course for USN test pilots so that they may experience the torque from the powerful Merlin engine.

It is not only piston-engine aircraft that are being replicated and rebuilt: there is a healthy warbird jet population. As this book was going to press, details were emerging of a new project being undertaken by Classic Fighter Industries in conjunction with the Texas Airplane Company of Fort Worth. The project involves the building of four Me 262s, essentially brand new though containing some original parts. To overcome the unreliability of the stock Jumo engine, Learjet engines are being used. The purchase price of each aircraft will be some $1.2 million and two-seat as well as single-seat configurations will be produced. In mid-1993 this company rolled out four Grumman F3F 'flying barrels' which are now to be seen in the air regularly.

Not only is the warbird world alive and well, it is expanding, bringing to the attention of the public the classic and beautiful aircraft of the Second World War that shaped the course of aviation.

Theatres of the Air

Philip Handleman/Tim Laming

Fittingly, the undisputed Mecca of aviation thrives amid the dairy farms and cornfields of Midwestern America. During the first week of August every year, near the usually placid shores of Wisconsin's Lake Winnebago, the sky fills with the welcome rattle of sparklingly restored, radial-engine aeroplanes. In the quaint town of Oshkosh, with its Victorian-style clapboard homes, neat lawns and colourful flower boxes, the stalwart Experimental Aircraft Association hosts the world's largest annual aviation event – the EAA's Convention and Fly-In, which, by tradition, is universally referred to simply as 'Oshkosh'. In

Left: The main entrance to the Oshkosh convention grounds, looking west, is festooned with the flags of some of the countries represented by the many international visitors. In the background, centre, is Wittman Field's control tower. (Philip Handleman)

Right: Oshkosh's show-case taxiway displays airliners and Second World War bombers next to Korean War jets and fighters from today's arsenals. (Nicholas Veronico)

Below: This Short Sunderland was recently imported into the United States by Kermit Weeks. The first stop was the Oshkosh Fly-In, the boat landing on Lake Winnebago. (Nicholas Veronico)

Fly Past, Fly Present

Right: The mirror pass is the signature act in the routine flown by the peripatetic aerobatic team known as the French Connection. *Flying CAP 10B trainers, the two pilots are noted for bringing their aeroplanes extremely close in an amazing display of precision. (Philip Handleman)*

Below: Occupying a special place by the Antique/Classic 'red barn' at Oshkosh in 1993 was this glistening 1933 De Havilland DH 83 Fox Moth. The story of how it arrived at the fly-in and then returned home could make a book in itself. Owner and pilot Roger Fiennes, a Londoner, contracted for a New Zealand aircraft restoration company to rebuild the old DH. It was then shipped to Oakland, California, where Fiennes began an aerial odyssey across America to Oshkosh. After the show he flew on to New Jersey and then sailed home to England aboard the Queen Elizabeth II *with his prized possession stored in the ship's cargo hold. (Philip Handleman)*

Right: In 1989 the Red Baron Stearman Squadron included Oshkosh in its very busy schedule. Equipped with 450-horsepower Pratt & Whitney engines and constant-speed propellers, this unique four-ship formation makes an ear-splitting racket during its low-level performances. With their speed built up, the Stearmans arch upwards in formation and then cascade gracefully downwards to close the loop. (Philip Handleman)

Below: Few aircraft conjure up the thrilling images of aviation's Golden Age – those breathtaking years between the world wars – as effectively as the 1930s racing aeroplanes. In those days the great Jimmy Doolittle swept the board at the Cleveland Air Races in the stub-wing Gee Bee. Produced by the Granville brothers, the Gee Bee was conceived as a record-breaking speedster; it proved to be so, but it was difficult to control and the few that were built ended their days in crashes. However, at his Montana farm, intrepid air show pilot Delmar Benjamin built a replica of the Gee Bee R-2 and since unveiling his creation has wowed millions with his hair-rasing aerobatic routine. (Philip Handleman)

the course of the event more than 800,000 of the aviation faithful flock to Wittman Regional Airport. Homebuilders, 'antiquers' and warbirds occupy distinct sections of the airport grounds, dedicated to showcasing their respective categories of aircraft.

From shortly after sunrise to well after sunset, myriad forums are conducted under circus-like tents, ranging in subject matter from the reminiscences of veteran racing pilots to the latest satellite-based navigation systems on the market. There are regularly scheduled 'hands-on' workshops in fabric covering, metalwork and welding. Vendors from across the land gather to offer their wares to throngs of aviation enthusiasts in spacious buildings and in an ever-expanding open-air 'fly market'. All the while, aeroplanes of every shape and size, and from every era of aviation's rich history, cre-

ate a constant panoramic flow in Wittman Field's traffic pattern, providing continuous entertainment for those who choose to sit back in garden chairs or recline on blankets thrown over the grass.

Officials allocate the afternoon airspace to the formal flying displays, and over the years Oshkosh has emerged as one of the premier events for the world's leading air show performers. Probably no other show features such a diverse mixture of pilots and aircraft. The supersonic Concorde may make a couple of low-level passes after a Pitts has completed a stomach-churning aerobatic routine, and a formation of Marine Corps Harriers may ascend vertically before a husband-and-wife wing-walking team puts on a heart-stopping act in a vintage, open-cockpit biplane.

At Oshkosh, many of the vaunted names from aviation's past resurface and take on a tangible quality among the multitudinous rows of parked aircraft in the Antique/Classic area. The adventure of the formative years really comes back to life.

The European Scene

The United Kingdom can lay claim to some of the world's most congested airspace, which is hardly surprising when one considers the size of the British Isles relative to the huge demand for business, leisure and military usage of the islands' skies. It is probably very fortunate, therefore, that many British citizens, young and old, seem to have an unusually keen interest in aircraft. Why this should be so is unclear: it may be a reflection of the country's historical connections with aviation, or it may be another example of British eccentricity! Whatever the reasons, there is ample evidence of this national obsession with aircraft. Every summer there is a staggering list of aviation events, ranging from small 'garden party' gatherings to the huge International Air Tattoo where hundreds of military aeroplanes come together. There is no doubt that, for the air show addict, Britain is *the* place to be!

The British air show scene has certainly changed significantly since the pre-First World War gathering of biplanes and balloons at Doncaster Racecourse in Yorkshire – the first 'air show'. Every year the calendar of events grows and diversifies: in 1993, for example, more than 200 organized shows took place during the period from April to October. Many of these events are small, with a distinctly local audience, and gatherings of private aircraft ('fly-ins'), balloon meets and trade and industry displays take place regularly throughout the year but rarely attract large crowds. The main British events, however, form the basis of a fairly small list of regular display venues, to which many thousands of enthusiasts and casual observers return year after year to enjoy a close look at the objects of their interest and affection and to talk to the people who maintain and fly them.

The most famous event in Britain is, of course, the biennial Society of British Aerospace Companies show held at the Defence Research Agency's airfield at Farnborough. Having grown from a relatively small annual display of British aviation products, the SBAC show is now a major international event, attracting civil and military trade representatives from around the world, together with the latest aircraft designs, and hundreds of thousands of spectators. The Royal Air Force, as part of its continuing policy to maintain good public relations, stages annual open days around the United Kingdom. The most ambitious RAF events have traditionally been the Battle of Britain 'At Home' days, which were organized by many stations throughout the country, especially during the immediate post-war years. However, only two stations, Finningley – which is scheduled for closure – and Leuchars, now hold annual 'At Home' days, although some stations do arrange 'air days' on a less regu-

Above: This beautifully restored De Havilland Venom is one of a growing number of former Swiss Air Force Venoms and Vampires appearing at air shows around the world. (Tim Laming)

Right: The fascinating sight of a 'Bear' and a 'Midas' together at the 1993 International Air Tattoo. Who could ever have imagined, a few years ago, that a Russian strategic bomber would appear at an air show in Britain? (Tim Laming)

Right: The all-too-rare appearances in Britain of Switzerland's Patrouille Suisse *were hugely popular, no doubt because of the RAF's long association with the Hunter. Although the team ended its operations with Hunters in 1994, the type continues to appear at air shows in civilian-owned warbird guise. (Tim Laming)*

lar basis. As military resources continue to dwindle, the number of RAF shows has fallen considerably, and as stations continue to be closed down the situation is unlikely to improve.

Across the English Channel, the European air show scene has also begin to change, although it is fair to say that no European country has ever matched the scale of Britain's obsession with air shows. The post-Cold War reduction in military spending has had a drastic effect on the structure of every military air arm, but smaller nations such as Belgium and the Netherlands have been particularly eager to make big cut-backs in expenditure, leading to the withdrawal of many front-line aircraft and the closure of many bases. Naturally, there has been a corresponding drop in the number of base open days, although, as in Britain,

smaller civilian-organized events continue to take place. In Germany air shows have virtually disappeared following the disaster at Ramstein when aircraft from Italy's *Il Frecce Tricolori* collided in front of thousands of horrified onlookers, killing pilots and spectators.

However, as the number of big military shows declines, the number of civilian-organized events continues to remain high. The most ambitious 'civil' event is, oddly enough, now the world's biggest military air show! The International Air Tattoo has now become the highlight of the annual calendar, attracting hundreds of aircraft from around the world and truly phenomenal numbers of spectators, many of whom are happy to spend three or four days, or more, watching the massive show come together and disperse. Unlike the organizers of almost every

other air show, the IAT Committee actively caters for the interests of aircraft enthusiasts rather than just the general public. Great efforts are made to gather together rare and interesting aircraft, and enthusiasts are given every opportunity to see each aircraft at close quarters, even on days prior to and after the show weekend. Few could offer anything but praise for the organizers of this outstanding event, although some might suggest that the IAT has become *too* big, as the flying display continues to expand from year to year. The organizers have now been forced to restrict some demonstrations to only one of the two main days – an unpopular move as far as the spectators are concerned, but, as the IAT Committee points out, the flying would continue into the night if everyone were to display on both days! Perhaps the Committee will eventually be forced to 'weed out' some of the displays which are common to many other shows in Britain, in order to devote time to the more interesting exhibits, or perhaps the two-day event will have to be spread over a three-day holiday weekend. Certainly, the number of exotic exhibits at each IAT has remained surprisingly high, despite the gradual disappearance of rare and unusual aircraft from the world's military air arms. The 1993 event, for example, brought a Russian Tu-95 'Bear' to Britain for the first time, fascinating thousands of enthusiasts over the show weekend. Following the outstanding success of each IAT, one is left to wonder what exciting show-stopper will appear at the next event!

Individual displays by front-line military aircraft may become a thing of the past if budget restrictions force the RAF to withdraw from air show participation. Ironically, this may encourage the Ministry of Defence to retain the *Red Arrows*, whose future has been the subject of speculation, in order to maintain a Royal Air Force presence at shows in Europe and elsewhere. It may well be that the emphasis in air shows shifts from military to civilian participation: as more and more military aircraft are retired or withdrawn, the number of aircraft – particularly relatively modern aircraft – being restored to airworthy condition by civilians continues to increase.

Although Second World War aircraft have been the subject of restoration projects for many years, the interest in later-generation aircraft, especially jets, is on the increase. The United States was the leader in this field with such types as the F-86 Sabre appearing at air shows, and in Britain aircraft like the Hunter, and now the Canberra and Lightning, are candidates for preservation. In Europe, France has so far been the only country to see such work, with aircraft such as the Vautour and Mystère taking to the air in warbird guise. With the immensely popular Avro Vulcan being considered for active air show participation under civilian ownership, it seems that even the most complex and expensive aeroplanes can be restored, maintained and safely operated. For the future, there seems to be every possibility that types like the Buccaneer, F-104, Phantom and Draken may also be 'civilianized' and flown. The passion of enthusiasts and general public for aviation looks likely to be satisfied for many years to come!

Why Preserve?

Walter Boyne/Don Storer

In a civilization that reveres Tutankhamen, Mayan temples, Charlie Chaplin films and 'sightings' of Elvis Presley, enquiring why we should preserve aeroplanes is absurd. Just as the *Victory* and the *Constitution* are examples of the means by which, respectively, Great Britain and the United States achieved greatness in the eighteenth century, and as the great railway museums represent the achievements of the nineteenth, so do aircraft collectively and individually represent the best and brightest of the twentieth. Some might raise the red herrings of automobiles or (God forbid!) the computer, and ask why these should not be preserved as well. The answer, of course, is that they should, by those who wish to do so, and for many of the same reasons as those given below.

There are both subjective and objective reasons for preserving aircraft. Most of us are governed by the subjective reasons, which are at the same time the most urgent and the least cogent. The objective reasons are more rational, less passionate, but utterly convincing. Combined, they put the imprimatur of common sense upon the great movement that we enjoy today and which grew in many of our lifetimes from a hesitant, almost eccentric hobby for a few to an international movement that commands hundreds of millions of dollars' worth of investment and requires the input of hundreds of thousands of man-hours by highly skilled craftsmen.

Subjectively, the need to preserve aircraft stems from the affectionate relationship they inspire in the *cognoscenti*, those already aware of the glamour and importance of aircraft in general and who are usually interested in a special type of aircraft in particular. Find a crew member from the Eighth Air Force and ask him how he regards the Boeing B-17; talk to a woman who served as a stewardess on a Constellation and ask her how she feels about the 'Connie'; or take an old-time flight instructor aside and let him tell you what he thinks of the Stearman or Tiger Moth or Stampe. Each person will respond with convincing stories of why his or her aeroplane is important.

Left, upper: This Hawker Fury is ex-Iraqi N666HP, which was rebuilt at Breckenbridge Aviation Museum. (William Jesse)
Left, lower: A Grumman FM-2 Wildcat, restored over many years by Antiques and Classics Inc., based in Illinois. The Wildcat was, with the Hellcat, an important player in the Pacific theatre during the Second World War. (William Jesse)
Below: One of many examples flying, this North American T-6 carries the unmistakable yellow training colour scheme. (William Jesse)

But one does not have to be a pilot or a crew member to have these same subjective feelings, for there are counterparts for each of the above. The same sense of regard for the B-17 was inspired in the villagers living around the Eighth Air Force bases, who watched the daily departures of orderly formations and then waited, breathless for their sometimes less orderly return. In a similar way, hundreds of thousands of passengers found the 'Connie' a delight: there was something soothing about an unhurried, eight-hour flight across the country when you had plenty of room to stretch out and the stewardess had time enough to be genuinely concerned about you. And for everyone who flew in a trainer, there were a dozen children hanging on the fence, watching, vicariously feeling the wind in their faces and the rapid movements of stick and rudder pedal on the touch-down.

These are but three examples; they could be expanded several thousandfold, to encompass the experience and dreams of the millions of people who over the last century have had their lives affected by aircraft and aviation. Some of the most fervent in the movement are those who have had a father or a mother involved in aviation and who have appropriated their parents' interests. Others, equally involved, had no close connection at all with the object of their desire but may only have made a model of it once, or have seen it represented in a film or depicted in a magazine.

These are subjective reasons, and they alone are ample to preserve aircraft. A whole population of individuals exists

for whom a Mustang is more beautiful than a Rembrandt, a Spitfire lovelier than a Cezanne, a Thunderbolt more voluptuous than a Renoir. An incontrovertible argument could be made for the preservation of great art solely on the basis that people appreciate its beauty: the fact that it is the currency of a culture could be totally ignored, and keeping the paintings would still be justified. Exactly the same argument can be made for restoring aircraft: they are objects of transcendent beauty and deserve to be presented as they were when they were earning their keep in the air. But, as we shall see, aircraft are far more the currency of our culture than is any art, for while a work of art is an expression of individual genius, an aircraft is the product of an extended team that ranges from the inspired de-

Left: A Vultee Valiant trainer of the US Army Air Corps. Designed originally as a private venture, the Valiant became the most numerous USAAF trainer of the Second World War. (William Jesse)

Below: With its distinctive overall white paint scheme and striking red markings, this Yakovlev Yak-11 first flew in restored form in 1991. (William Jesse)

signer to the rivet-bucker and the supply sergeant chasing parts for it.

The objective reasons are less aesthetic but even more compelling. Aircraft are more than achievements of our century: they are icons of living history, each one a snapshot of the people, the technology, the mathematics, the science of its time. As a single example, imagine a class of students who, while very bright, have never seen or heard an aeroplane. Take as an example any aircraft at random – for the purposes of this argument, let us make it a Hurricane. Place a Hurricane in the classroom with students of any nation – the United States, Great Britain, Germany, Russia – and then see what a marvellous curriculum can be developed.

In the hands of any reasonably competent instructor, the Hurricane – or,

again, any aeroplane from the Wright Flyer to the Space Shuttle – could be a point of departure for delving into the pure sciences – mathematics, physics, chemistry, thermodynamics – for each of these disciplines was vital to its creation. The study would also lead to an examination of applied sciences – metallurgy, hydraulics, pneumatics, electricity, aerodynamics and ballistics for starters. The little fighter would open the doors to history, moving backwards to the story of Tom Sopwith, Harry Hawker and the beginnings of military aviation and the First World War; and forwards through time to Sidney Camm, the Battle of Britain, North Africa, and Middle East and Asia, and then to follow-on designs like the great Hunter and John Fozard's Harrier.

That would be for openers. Then there would come the question of who designed the Hurricane and what the requirements were. What was the political situation that demanded a changeover from the silver biplanes that flew on sunny afternoons to a menacing eight-gun camouflaged monoplane that fought in every theatre of war? Who was clever enough to demand an eight-gun armament anyway? Why was the development of propellers delayed so that controllable-pitch units, available for years, had quickly to be retrofitted in the field? What portion of the national income did it take to set up the factories and train the workforce to put the aircraft into production?

Think of the cultural questions the Hurricane raises! How much were workers paid? What were the working conditions like in Britain compared to those in France or the United States? When did

women come into the workforce to build the aircraft? Did shareholders exploit the workers or the government? What might have been done to improve the factory environment? What was the effect of the factory on the environment?

Carrying things a step further, what were the labour skills involved? Of mixed construction, the Hurricane required skilled woodworkers, pattern-makers, die-makers, metal workers, fabric experts, painters ≈ what is the history of their skills? How did they conduct their opera-

tions so as to be swift and economic? How did they live, what did they wear, what did they eat, what did they do for amusement, what were their standards of morality – in short, who *were* these thousands of people who contributed to the Hurricane and what is their relevance today? The questions go on and on. The Hurricane, as any aircraft could, embraces the whole history of our culture, science, politics, engineering, every aspect of our lives, and therefore deserves to be preserved, studied and admired.

Left: While having long ceased aircraft production, the Ryan Aeronautical Company has to its credit such renowned aircraft as the NYP, better known as the Spirit of St Louis. *In the 1930s Ryan also produced this two-seat sport monoplane, the STM. With war on the horizon, primary trainers were needed and, not unexpectedly, Ryan entered the field with the PT-22 Recruit, a design that drew from the STM. (Philip Handleman)*

Right, top: Restored aircraft come in all shapes and sizes and include unusual subjects such as light observation/liaison aircraft for USAAF/US Army co-operation duties. (William Jesse)

Right, centre: A new Spitfire fuselage out of the jig: Eddie Coventry's low-back Mk XVI, finished in an eye-catching red and silver paint scheme. (Paul Coggan/Warbirds World-wide)

Right, bottom: This example of the rugged Douglas AD Skyraider has had a busy history since its release for civilian use in 1960, including time with the Armée de l'Air, *recovery from Gabon in 1976 and transport to the USA via Dublin to its current flying status. (William Jesse)*

Fly Past, Fly Present

Thus the single best reason for preserving aircraft, past, present and future, is that each one furnishes a snapshot of its own time, offering a significant commentary on the contemporary state of science, commerce, art and war. At first blush this may seem a pretentious statement, but it is instead portentous, for it points to the future need to 'humanize' the achievements of the twentieth century in a manner that will be easily understood in the twenty-first and beyond. The world is changing rapidly, and, as cultural values shift, it is important to have some tangible benchmarks of past achievements available for inspiration, motivation and education. Every aircraft preserved and restored represents a hundred disciplines that range from basic engineering, through the procurement and testing of materials, to the creation of specialized tools. To this end we must mourn the aeroplanes that will never be restored since none exists – as far as we know. It would be marvellous to have a Martin GMB, a Douglas B-19, a McDonnell XP-67 or a Berliner-Joyce P-16 to see and study. Fortunately, the preservation movement has reached a point when fantastic reproductions like those of Jim Appleby, Carl Swanson and Herb Tischler can recreate aeroplanes that have long been lost from view. Add to these the teams that keep Blenheims, Lancasters, Liberators, Mustangs, B-29s and all the rest flying, and we can be confident that

Below: One of the treats that comes with attending a fly-in as large as that at Oshkosh is the inevitability of rare aeroplanes being on view. True to form, in 1993 a pair of exotic Davis D-1W parasol monoplanes turned up. This vermilion and yellow example was built in 1935 and was restored by its current owners, Jack and Kate Tiffany, whose hard work was acknowledged with an EAA restoration award. Note the meticulous attention to detail, such as the fuselage trim stripe repeated on the wheel fairings. (Philip Handleman)

our heritage is being properly transmitted, that what was given to us by our predecessors will be passed on to those who follow.

Preservation in Britain

People collect and preserve all manner of things for a variety of good reasons. Some people are just avid collectors and enjoy the process of collecting, be it stamps, matchboxes or aircraft. For others, collecting is merely a means to an end: they enjoy using their old gramophones or flying their vintage aeroplanes. And there are those who feel strongly that it is important to preserve our heritage, that much-used word which the dictionary defines, unhelpfully, as 'that which may be or is inherited'. Our heritage can be viewed in a number of different ways, from pure nostalgia to social history, showing life as it was – 'warts an' all'. It

could also be considered from a technical angle, to show how Concorde evolved from the Wright Flyer. Realistically, no collector can collect without a degree of selectivity, especially if the objects are large, expensive and difficult to preserve – such as aircraft. Collectors aiming to preserve our aviation heritage range from enthusiastic amateurs to professional museum curators.

If we accept the fact that we cannot preserve everything, then we are faced with a selection process – what to preserve and what to scrap? This is a dilemma which can induce a headache whichever choice is made. In many cases the selection has been made for us by our predecessors and we have inherited their decisions – decisions which all too often were not made consciously. For example, during the Second World War the Handley Page Halifax was used by the thousand, but not a single example was preserved: there was no conscious selection process at the end of the war. Some aircraft have been preserved because of the efforts of individuals or groups, while others have been ignored. With hindsight, we should have preserved at least one example of each major aircraft type. We did not, and thus our museums have had to go to great lengths to make good this omission. The RAF Museum recovered an almost complete Halifax from a Norwegian lake, but this presented them with enormous problems of conservation and restoration.

Historic aircraft which have survived have often done so more by accident than by design. True, one or two museums made a conscious effort between the wars and there have been a handful of private collectors, who, it has to be said, were looked upon as being rather eccentric at the time. Luckily, the collections of Richard Shuttleworth and R. G. J. Nash have survived, the former at Old Warden and the latter at the Royal Air Force Museum, Hendon. Many early aircraft have survived because they were originally stored away, in a hangar roof or in a barn, and forgotten. One must bear in mind that surviving antiques have had to pass through a dangerous 'throwaway' period: once an item has ceased to be used, because it is worn out or no longer in fashion, it is in danger. During this period it is not yet considered to be worth collecting so it is disposed of, or, with luck, put to one side.

Even as late as the 1950s there were no significant aircraft museums in Britain. The Science Museum and the Imperial War Museum exhibited some aircraft as part of their comprehensive displays, but there was no Royal Air Force Museum nor Fleet Air Arm Museum. The total number of preserved aircraft on static display was probably under 100. The turning point came in 1960, when there was a sudden surge in the preservation of aircraft, not instigated by the museum professionals but by enthusiastic amateurs. One of the first successes was the Mosquito Aircraft Museum at Salisbury Hall in Hertfordshire, which opened in 1959 to display the prototype Mosquito at the place where it was designed. The first large, purely aeronautical museum in Britain was another private venture: the Skyfame Aircraft Museum in Gloucestershire contained many interesting exhibits, and these, despite the subsequent financial collapse of the concern, have survived.

In 1967 the British Aircraft Preservation Council (BAPC) was formed by ten organizations, of which eight were private ventures and two, the RAF Museum and the Fleet Air Arm Museum, national institutions. Ten years later the BAPC had 48 full member organizations preserving aircraft and ten associate members; the number of aircraft being preserved was about 500. The BAPC has now become the British Aviation Preservation Council to reflect a growing interest in preservation on a wider front, including airfields, radar equipment, weapons, radio equipment, uniforms and vehicles associated with airfields. Today there are 115 full and 27 associate members. The number of aircraft preserved in Britain is now well over 1,000, including those of non-BAPC members, and of this figure

fewer than half are preserved in buildings. To maintain a large aircraft in reasonably good condition when it is kept outside is an expensive operation. Sums of £10,000 to £20,000 a year have been quoted, but, of course, volunteer workers cut these costs dramatically.

Almost all aircraft need some conservation or restoration when first acquired, even if they have come straight out of service. The first major dilemma is, to fly or not to fly? Obviously, restoration to flying condition is very much more expensive than for static display. Approved materials have to be used, inspections carried out and so on. But there is a moral issue: if the aircraft is famous and rare, should it be risked in the air? The classic example of this dilemma was provided by the one and only Bristol Bulldog fighter of the 1930s which was flown: it crashed at Farnborough in 1964, and now we do not have a Bulldog. (The RAF Museum are hoping to build a Bulldog using the surviving fragments, but this will be more of a replica than the real thing.)

Restoring an aircraft – especially a wood and fabric aircraft – may involve the replacement of damaged parts, but if

Left, upper: If the sight of the venerable Shackleton were not enough to stir an air show crowd, then the sound never failed to impress. The RAF's Shackletons have now passed into retirement but two examples await restoration to flying condition at Coventry, although their future is uncertain. In Cyprus, however, a Shackleton has already taken to the air in civilian hands. (Tim Laming)
Left, lower: Built for service in Europe in the Second World War, the A-26 continued to fly with the USAF and in 1958 was developed into the B-26 Invader, which served with success in South-East Asia. (William Jesse)

too many parts are replaced it becomes a hybrid or a semi-replica, a reduced standard in terms of 'original content'. Restoration to flying condition demands more replacements than for static display, so the percentage of original content must be reduced. One solution to this problem is to keep one representative of each type as a master (a 'type specimen', in natural history parlance), then fly any others – with care. Building replicas to fly is an excellent alternative. Some are little more than wolves in sheep's clothing, but others are constructed as near as possible to the specification of the original aircraft – same engine, same materials and so on.

The work of restoration plays an important part in preserving our heritage, not only by rejuvenating old aircraft but also by keeping alive some of the skills of the aircraft builders. From the early wood and fabric construction to steel-tube frameworks, and then aluminium alloy shells, the processes evolved. Modern aircraft may employ titanium, plastics and parts shaped by computer-controlled machinery. The aircraft industry has always been at the forefront of technical innovation, but the size of the industry has declined in recent years. This makes the preservation of old skills even more of a priority if future generations are to understand the past, when manual skills were all important. Luckily, more and more museums are training young people to develop these manual skills and, more important, are allowing visitors to watch the work of restoration as it progresses. The cost of a restoration can be very high: a typical project might consume £100,000 inclusive of man-hours and materials. There is no doubt that aircraft in the air are an attractive sight, but many people also enjoy a closer inspection on the ground, perhaps even seeing the interior of the subject – not only getting the 'feel' of it but also, in some cases, the unique smell.

It is unlikely that very many more aircraft will be preserved in Britain since new candidates rarely appear and fewer collectable aircraft are coming out of service. The cost of looking after existing aircraft is another factor limiting the growth in numbers. Museums are building hangars to allow their aircraft to be moved indoors and so enable their lives to be extended. If it proves impossible to maintain all the preserved aircraft, then a grading system would be advantageous in order to divert funds (especially Government grants) to the most deserving cases. The BAPC is co-operating with other bodies to produce such a list, similar to the existing system of 'listing' buildings deemed worthy of protection.

The main aim of the collectors should be to fill the gaps where no known example of a classic aircraft survives. Replicas provide a solution of course, especially for aircraft that are going to be flown, but high costs tend to rule out this option where large aircraft are concerned. Unfortunately, these are generally the ones missing from the existing collections: for example, there is no surviving Stirling bomber of the Second World War. Static display aircraft can sometimes be built from the remains of a crashed aircraft, however, examples here being a Wellington, a Whitley, a Barracuda and of course the Halifax already mentioned.

Above: Denmark's Saab Drakens have gone from front-line service but a small number have been sold to civilian buyers in the United States and may well reappear as warbirds in due course. (Tim Laming)
Right: One of the highlights of the 1993 International Air Tattoo was the first appearance in Britain of Hungarian Air Force MiG-21 fighters. (Tim Laming)

Why Preserve?

To assure the future of our preserved aircraft we have to make good use of them by entertaining and educating the public. Flying displays offer entertainment and excitement; static displays can educate and still be entertaining. Modern display techniques can provide living history lessons, as pioneered so successfully by the Jorvik Viking Centre in York. Aviation museums offer a range of 'experience' exhibitions; for example, the RAF Museum presents 'Battle of Britain', 'On Target', 'The Friendly Invasion', 'The Dambusters' and a modern flight simulator offering visitors a 'sortie' in a Tornado. There is a 'hands-on' interactive display, 'Flight Lab', at the Science Museum, while the Imperial War Museum presents 'The Blitz Experience' at Lambeth and 'Dawn Patrol' at Duxford.

The Authors

Walter J. Boyne's prize-winning writing combines the enthusiasm of the life-long 'buff', the accuracy of a distinguished historian, the experience of a 4,000-hour military pilot and the broad knowledge derived from his work as Director of Smithsonian's National Air and Space Museum. He is one of the few people to have had both fiction and non-fiction books on the *New York Times*' best-seller list. His most recent book, *Clash of Wings*, the story of the great air campaigns of the Second World War, has received wide acclaim. He has written 25 books and 400 articles and does extensive *pro bono* consultancy work with aviation writers.

Born in Shirebrook, Derbyshire, **Paul Coggan** had his first brush with aviation at the age of six, when he began to keep a logbook of aircraft flying over his area. On leaving school he joined the Royal Air Force and his chosen field of Air Traffic Control, but in his spare time he formed an organization for Mustang enthusiasts and began publishing a newsletter called *Mustang International*. In only a few years this had turned into a 25-page magazine, the forerunner of the now very popular *Warbirds Worldwide Journal*. In 1986 he resigned from the RAF to concentrate on his publishing work, which now includes the editorship of the triennial *Warbirds Worldwide Directory*. In 1991 he was appointed Historic Aircraft Consultant to Sotheby's in London, and he also acts as Consultant in aviation matters to Edgar Hamilton Aviation, Lloyd's Insurance Brokers, in London. As well as being a prolific writer he also undertakes consultancy work for private individuals seeking warbird aircraft.

Colin Dodds learned to fly at the age of seventeen, holding a pilot's licence before obtaining his driving licence. He served in the Royal Air Force, flying Vulcans, HS 125s and Nimrods, interspersed with staff appointments. Since leaving the RAF as a senior officer in 1982, he has been associated with many aspects of the vintage aircraft movement, including in particular the De Havilland Moth Club. He has been involved in the restoration and operation of a number of historic machines, including Leopard Moth G-AIYS, Fox Moth G-AOJH and Dragon Rapide G-AEML. He now operates the Rapide on behalf of Proteus Petroleum and works in defence equipment marketing for British Aerospace's Systems and Services Division. He is Deputy Chairman of the Historic Aircraft Association, a CAA-authorized display pilot and a Display Authorization Evaluator.

Philip Handleman has enjoyed a life-long love affair with aviation. Since his first flight, in a Piper Cub, at the age of twelve, he has unstintingly pursued his interest in aeroplanes and flying. He has been a licensed pilot for more than 23 years, and he currently owns and flies two restored aircraft of military lineage, including an open-cockpit Stearman biplane. The author of six aviation books and many dozens of articles, he is a recognized aviation authority. For many years he has beautifully captured a wide range of aircraft in his still photography, and he is also President of Handleman Filmworks, an award-winning television production company that has produced highly acclaimed documentary programmes. He and his wife Mary divide their time between their home in Birmingham, Michigan, and a private airstrip in the nearby countryside.

Born in 1958 and educated near Southampton, **Peter Jacobs** joined the Royal Air Force in 1977 as a Technician Apprentice at RAF Halton. On completion of his training he was accepted for officer training at the RAF College at Cranwell; he was commissioned in 1981 and he completed his navigator training and was posted to the F-4 Phantom at Coningsby in 1983. Having completed a tour with No 29(F)

Squadron – during which time he served with No 23 Squadron in the Falkland Islands – he was posted to Finningley as a navigator instructor and in 1990 returned to Coningsby to serve as an instructor with the Tornado F.3 Operational Conversion Unit (later No 56 Squadron), during which time he spent a short period with the Battle of Britain Memorial Flight. He was promoted to Squadron Leader in 1993 and currently serves as the Air Defence Specialist at the Defence Research Agency in Farnborough. Married, with two young children, he is a keen RAF historian and has numerous articles to his credit. He has enjoyed recent success with his first book, *The Six-Year Offensive*.

William Jesse has had a love of aircraft for as long as he can remember. He had spent most of his adult life working in the aviation industry and, besides writing and taking photographs for various aviation magazines around the world, he is the Canadian contributor to *FlyPast* magazine and a regular feature writer for *The Atlantic Flyer*. He currently resides in Victoria, British Columbia.

Aged 32, **Tim Laming** developed an interest in aviation during early childhood. After leaving school he worked as a civil servant, though he pursued his hobby of aviation photography in his spare time and began contributing features to journals such as *Scale Models*, *Aviation News* and *Aircraft Illustrated*. His first book was published by Ian Allan, and this was followed by a photographic essay entitled *Flying Tankers* for Osprey. During the early 1980s he began working full time as a freelance writer and photographer and was appointed Editor of *Skywarriors* magazine. He has written books for publishers such as Airlife, Virgin and Arms & Armour Press. He lives in Sheffield but travels in pursuit of aircraft whenever possible.

Bob Ogden became interested in aircraft whilst at school and made several cycle tours of airfields and museums in Britain, France and Belgium in the 1950s. He has visited museums throughout Europe and the United States and in several countries in Asia. He was Chairman of the Midland Preservation Society and of the British Aircraft Preservation Council from 1968 to 1970, and he was the Associate Editor of *Vintage Aircraft Magazine* from 1978 to 1982. He has written many articles for aviation magazines and also a number of books on museums, including the *Aircraft Museums and Collections of the World* series. He has restored a number of vintage aircraft, including a BAC Drone and a De Havilland Moth Minor. At the time of writing one of the few surviving DH Moth Majors is in his workshop.

After qualifying as a Mechanical Engineer at Imperial College, **J. D. Storer** spent eighteen years in the Design Office of Vickers-Armstrongs (later the British Aircraft Corporation) at Weybridge, working on aircraft from the Viscount to the Concorde. In 1966 he moved to the Royal Scottish Museum in Edinburgh, where he was largely responsible for setting the Museum of Flight at East Fortune Airfield. He retired from the Museum in 1988 and now works as a consultant and author. He has been on the Executive Committee of the British Aircraft Preservation Council for many years and is currently its Honorary Secretary.

Nicholas A. Veronico is an accomplished writer and photographher and a life-long aviation enthusiast. His primary interest is in US Navy aircraft of the 1940s and 1950s. His most recent books include *Wreck Chasing: A Guide to Finding Crash Sites* and *Vought F4U Corsair*. He currently serves as Editor of *Airliners* magazine and is a regular contributor to *FlyPast* magazine. He lives with his wife Pam and children Mark and Kim in Castro Valley, California.